The

Lancashire Witch

New Zealand Immigration Ship 1856–1867

By Belinda Lansley

Ancestral Journeys of New Zealand Series

This book would not have been possible without the help of the following people. Special thanks to:

Julian Hight, for use of the *Lancashire Witch* contract ticket

NZ Fine Prints for the use of the *Lancashire Witch* picture.

Marolyn Diver for her ongoing support

Olwyn at South Canterbury NZGenWeb Project, for permission to use the transcribed diaries

Original text © Belinda Lansley 2013
Images © named individuals, institutions
All rights reserved
ISBN 978-0-473-25496-4

Cover Design by Stuart and Belinda Lansley
Cover picture: *The Lancashire Witch* by Thomas Dutton. *Lancashire Witch* image available as a print from NZ Fine Prints | Prints.co.nz

Dedicated to our ancestors who endured terrible times at sea.

Belinda Lansley

Contents

Introduction	7
The Ship	9
Voyage to Wellington & Auckland 1856	25
Passengers to Wellington & Auckland 1856	31
Voyage to Timaru & Lyttelton 1863	35
Passengers to Timaru & Lyttelton 1863	65
Voyage to Auckland 1865	77
Passengers to Auckland 1865	89
Voyage to Lyttelton 1867	97
Passengers to Lyttelton 1867	121
Passenger Lists	125
References	*155*

Introduction

This book covers the history of a fascinating ship that sailed into Lyttelton and other ports around New Zealand. The name alone (which probably came from a terrible event in British history) almost jinxed this ship, and caused it some trouble. The ship even carried its own "Lancashire Witch" on board, transporting her into New Zealand to make trouble in the colony her whole life.

After initially thinking I had no connection to this ship whatsoever, I found the Dalton family came out on the *Lancashire Witch*. Thomas and Charlotte Dalton had a son Thomas Henry Dalton, who married my 3 x great aunt Emma Magdalena Meng. She was a much loved aunt in our family. It is funny how I have randomly picked ships and then discover a connection to me, if not a bit obscure.

I have obtained information for this book from original sources, but big thanks have to go to the keen genealogists who transcribed the diaries for the 1863 journey to New Zealand, which have been posted on Rootsweb. Using the diaries as a basis, I have written a cohesive story of the journey, using the three different points of view. It has been exciting to write and publish this account in 2013, the 150th anniversary of the 1863 journey!

If anyone has further information on the ship *Lancashire Witch* including ship diaries, family letters or comments in their family histories about the journey that you are willing to share, please contact me so it can be added to any future updated editions.

Belinda Lansley

belinda.lansley@yahoo.co.nz

The Ship

The *Lancashire Witch*

The *Lancashire Witch* was built in 1854 in Quebec, by shipbuilders Lomas and Sewell. It had the bust of a woman as a figurehead.[1] Whether this figurehead had a traditional witchlike appearance or not, is not mentioned in the records.

The Lancashire Witch – by Thomas Dutton (NZ Fine Prints: prints.co.nz)

The *Lancashire Witch* was built from oak and tamarac. It had a weight of 1383 tons[2] or 1386 tons[1] to begin with, which increased to 1574 tons[3] after modification of the ship. It had a burden of about 3500 tons.[4] The weight of burden was a good guide as to the maximum cargo allowed on board that would make the journey economic, as well as making sure the weight was not exceeded, which could cause the ship to sink while at sea.[5]

The *Lancashire Witch* was a clipper ship. The name "clipper ship" was a synonym for a merchant ship. They were first created by American ship builders in the 1840s and were extra fast, travelling on average 250 miles per day while other types of ships averaged 150 miles per day. English ship builders started to build them as well. They revolutionised sea transport and were wonderful ships to behold. Clipper ships had three masts and square sails, and it was this combination that made them so fast and popular in the 19th century.[5]

The Name *Lancashire Witch*

We can only presume that the name *Lancashire Witch* came from the story of twenty Lancashire people, mainly from Pendle Forest, who were trialled for witchcraft in Lancaster in 1612. Eight were acquitted, one died in jail and one was sentenced to stand in the pillory, but ten were hanged by the neck until dead. The court clerk Thomas Potts wrote about the trial and the book was called *The Wonderful Discovery of Witches in the county of Lancaster*. Another book, published in 1849 by Harrison Ainsworth, called *The Lancashire Witches,* popularised the subject in the 19th century, just before the ship *Lancashire Witch* was built in 1854. It was an imaginative novel, rather than a non-fiction piece. In 2012 it was the four hundred year anniversary of the witch hanging event and a modern English edition of Thomas Potts' book was published.[6] The term "Lancashire Witch" was also used in general language in the 19th century for a nasty or witch-like woman from Lancashire.

Because the *Lancashire Witch* had such a long name, passengers called her *The Witch* when referring to her in general conversation with other passengers or when reunions were documented in the newspapers.[7]

Other Ships named *Lancashire Witch*

It is important to note that there were other ships named *Lancashire Witch* at the time the clipper was sailing. This is probably because of the popular novel of the time. One was the brigantine *Lancashire Witch* which was sunk at sea in 1879 with all on board, through collision with the Spanish steamer Yrurac Bat.[8] The steamer didn't sink, just had broken bows.[9] Captain Hugh Edmonston was the sole survivor of this *Lancashire Witch*, with his crew below decks, failing to surface. He was picked up by the Yrurac Bat's lifeboat.[10]

Owners of the *Lancashire Witch*

The 1856 owners of the *Lancashire Witch* were D. Dunbar and Captain Molison when the first journey to New Zealand was made. In 1863 and 1865 for the second and third journeys it was G. Seymour of Seymour, Peacock & Co. The owner when the ship left London in 1867 was R. Kerr. Shaw, Savill & Co. chartered the vessel from the owners.

Shaw, Savill & Co.

Shaw, Savill & Co. ran a line of packet ships from Great Britain to New Zealand in the early years of colonisation. A packet ship was originally used for shipping post office mail to the colonies and other places around the world, but this meaning was eventually extended to include passengers as well as mail.[11] Shaw, Savill & Co. advertised regularly in English newspapers.

In 1854, the provincial governments became responsible for immigration. The Province of Canterbury had the largest immigration scheme of all the provinces, bringing in almost a fifth of all immigrants between 1858 and 1870. Two thirds of all passengers arriving in Canterbury were assisted; generally, half of their fare was paid by the Provincial Government.[12]

In 1863, Messrs. Shaw, Savill & co. secured the contract for carrying emigrants to Otago, the fares being £12 from Glasgow and £13 10s from London.[13] Rates for this journey, however, varied from £8[14] to £20[15] per person in steerage. The rates for steerage passengers on the *Lancashire Witch* were as follows:

	1863	1867
Single man or woman	£13 6s	£14
Couple	£26 12s	£28
Child	£6 13s	£7
Infant	free	free

For the *Clontarf* for the period of 1855–57, Willis Gann & Co. were charging £60 for one person in a chief cabin measuring 6 by 7ft, or £40 per person for two people sharing a cabin. The second cabins were 6ft 9in by 7ft 6in and for four people this cost £25 per person. Also available were second cabins for married couples measuring 3ft 6in by 7ft 8in at £25 per person.[14] Shaw, Savill & Co. would have charged more than this for cabins on the *Lancashire Witch*, being some years later. For the *Lancashire Witch* we only know the cost of a second cabin passenger on the 1867 voyage which was £30.[16]

The average annual wage for a housemaid in the 1850s–1860s was £11–£14.[17] Therefore, the full cost of the journey was a full year's wage. The average annual wage for a farm labourer in England and Wales in 1860 was £30 2s 4p[18], so the full cost of the journey was over a third of their annual wage. We can now see that travel to New Zealand was expensive and what a struggle it was to raise even half the fare. They often had help from family and friends already in the colony and, of course, the Provincial Government assisted by paying part of the fare.

In 1867 the 52 Single women on board the *Lancashire Witch* had their full fare paid by the Provincial Government. On arrival most of them already had positions in the colony. It was difficult to get good domestic servants to come to the colony, so by paying the whole fare they encouraged single women to come to New Zealand, thereby reducing the domestic servant shortage.

Shaw, Savill & Co. Contract Ticket

Amazingly a Contract Ticket for the Hight family who were on the 1863 *Lancashire Witch* journey has survived 150 years! A copy of it is on the next page. The food on board is listed for steerage passengers. The following statement is made above the food chart:

"The following quantities, at least of Water and Provisions (to be termed daily), will be supplied by the Master of the Ship, as required by Law, viz., to each Statute Adult Three Quarts of Water daily, and an additional Quart of Water daily while the Ship is within the Tropics, exclusive of what is necessary for cooking the articles required by the Passenger Act, to be issued in a cooked state, and a Weekly Allowance of Provisions according to the following scale:-

ARTICLES.		ARTICLES.	
Preserved Meats	1½ lb.	Butter	4 oz.
Soups and Bouilli	—	Cheese	6 oz.
York Hams	—	Currants	½ lb.
Fish	—	Raisins, Valentia	½ lb.
Salt Beef	1 lb.	Suet	8 oz.
—— Pork	1 lb.	Pickles	½ pt.
Biscuit	2lb. 10 oz.	Mustard	½ oz.
Flour	3½ lb.	Pepper	½ oz.
Rice or Oatmeal	1½ lb.	Salt	2 oz.
Barley	—	Potatoes, Fresh, or	3 lb.
Peas	½ pt.	Preserved ditto	½ lb.
Sugar, Raw	1 lb.	Molasses, West India	½ lb.
Lime Juice	6 oz.	Carrots	½ lb.
Tea	2 oz.	Celery Seed	½ oz.
Coffee, Roasted	8 oz.		

Food on the Hight family contract ticket. Lancashire Witch 1863 (detail).

The following is written under the above chart: "Children between one and four years of age are to receive Preserved Meat instead of Salt Meat every day, and in addition to the articles to which they are entitled by the above written scale, a quarter of a pint of Preserved Milk daily. Children under 1 year old, 3 pints of Water daily; and if above 4 months old, a quarter of a pint of Preserved Milk daily, and 3 ozs Preserved Soup, 12 ozs Biscuit, 4 ozs Oatmeal, 8 ozs Flour, 4 ozs Rice, and 10 ozs Sugar, weekly."

Cabin passengers usually had a slightly more varied diet than the chart shown, which was included in their more expensive ticket.

Hight family contract ticket. Lancashire Witch, 1863 (courtesy of Julian Hight).

The other interesting information from the contract ticket was that the luggage allowance on this journey in 1863 was twenty cubic feet for each statute adult.

Life on Board a Clipper Ship

According to some records, second cabin and steerage passengers were the only ones who received lime juice to keep away the scurvy with first class passengers not having to drink this concoction. Maybe the first class passengers received enough vitamin C from the more varied diet which included extra muscatel raisins and preserved carrots.[14] Records show that sometimes fowl were kept in coups for fresh eggs, and sometimes larger animals were kept on board for fresh meat. Water was stored in barrels but became stale and often grew algae or had vermin fall in and die. The *Lancashire Witch* had a large Graveley's distilling apparatus capable of serving out 600 gallons of water daily, and a first-rate steam cooking apparatus.[19] However the water distiller didn't work on the 1867 voyage, by the time they reached the tropics, and caused much discomfort for the passengers who were getting dehydrated. Food was stored in lidded barrels, but if someone left the lid off they could often become contaminated with rat and mice droppings. The bad hygiene often led to dysentery, cholera and many deaths on board. Flour often had weevils.

Illness was rife on some journeys, especially when steerage passengers were confined below decks during massive storms in the Southern Ocean. The ships were cleaned with vinegar and chloride of lime to remove vomit and make things smell better, while precious water was kept for drinking.

Toileting on ships was not pleasant. Often pieces of rag, soaked in vinegar, were hung on the back of the toilet door. These were used to wipe with and were shared over and over, often leading to dysentery! The sewage was often flushed into the bilge with buckets of water until emptied at port. The bilge was below steerage so the stench was not pleasant. People would be horrified these days but back then hygiene was not generally understood.[20] *Lancashire Witch* passenger Edgar Jones commented that he thought later generations were more virile due to better hygiene.[21]

The sleeping arrangements were bunk beds for steerage, with single women and single men having their own areas. Families often became separated, as most of the time children over the age of 12 were transferred to the single men's or single women's quarters. Bedding was aired in fine weather but often became soaked if water was coming into the ship; this led to influenza and pneumonia outbreaks.[20]

Some ships were better managed than others. The high death count on the 1863 *Lancashire Witch* voyage seemed to be more from bad luck more than bad management. The Captain and crew were outlined as being good people and there were no complaints made by passengers, in fact they were praising Dr Duncan McLean.[22]

On the more positive side, a ship journey such as this would have been one of life's biggest adventures for the emigrants. They would see and experience things they never dreamed of, including strange sea creatures, new constellations in the skies and a sea voyage which most would never repeat again in their lifetime, culminating in a strange new land at the final port. At night the passengers entertained each other with music, lectures of the new country and games, made new friends and contacts and looked forward to a brighter future in their new country.

Crew of a Clipper Ship

The average crew of a clipper ship without migrants was about 17, including the Captain, First Mate (or Chief Officer), Second Mate, Midshipman (Apprentice Officer), Ship's Carpenter, Boatswain, 9–10 ordinary seamen and the Cabin Boy who was used for mundane duties. There were usually two cooks: the Passenger's Cook who made food for the steerage passengers; and the Ship's Cook who catered for the more refined tastes of the cabin passengers and crew.

The crew numbers were closer to 40 when emigrants were on board, with additional crew including the Ship's Surgeon and Constable to keep the passenger welfare attended to. A Schoolmaster was on board to teach the children and a Matron to separate the single woman from the single men. Sometimes there was also a Minister on board. There were usually several Stewards, who looked after the Cabin Passengers. Some people took up a job on board to get free passage out.[23] The Matron, for example, was often a woman looking to emigrate, who took on the job in exchange for free passage.

Wages for the crew were on average £7 per month on the way to New Zealand with good food and comfortable accommodation but up to £100 wage total for the home journey, to ensure crew stuck with the ship and didn't desert once in New Zealand. Even with the better wage, desertions were common.[23]

On the 1863 journey of the *Lancashire Witch* it was mentioned that the crew got some extra perks. The Captain got 2/6 for each emigrant he delivered safely to New Zealand (called a gratuity). The First Mate got 1/- per head. The Cook made about 1 per month for the fat from the beef and pork. Also the passengers gave the Cook money for baking their bread beautifully, (2/6 was mentioned).[24]

The Ship

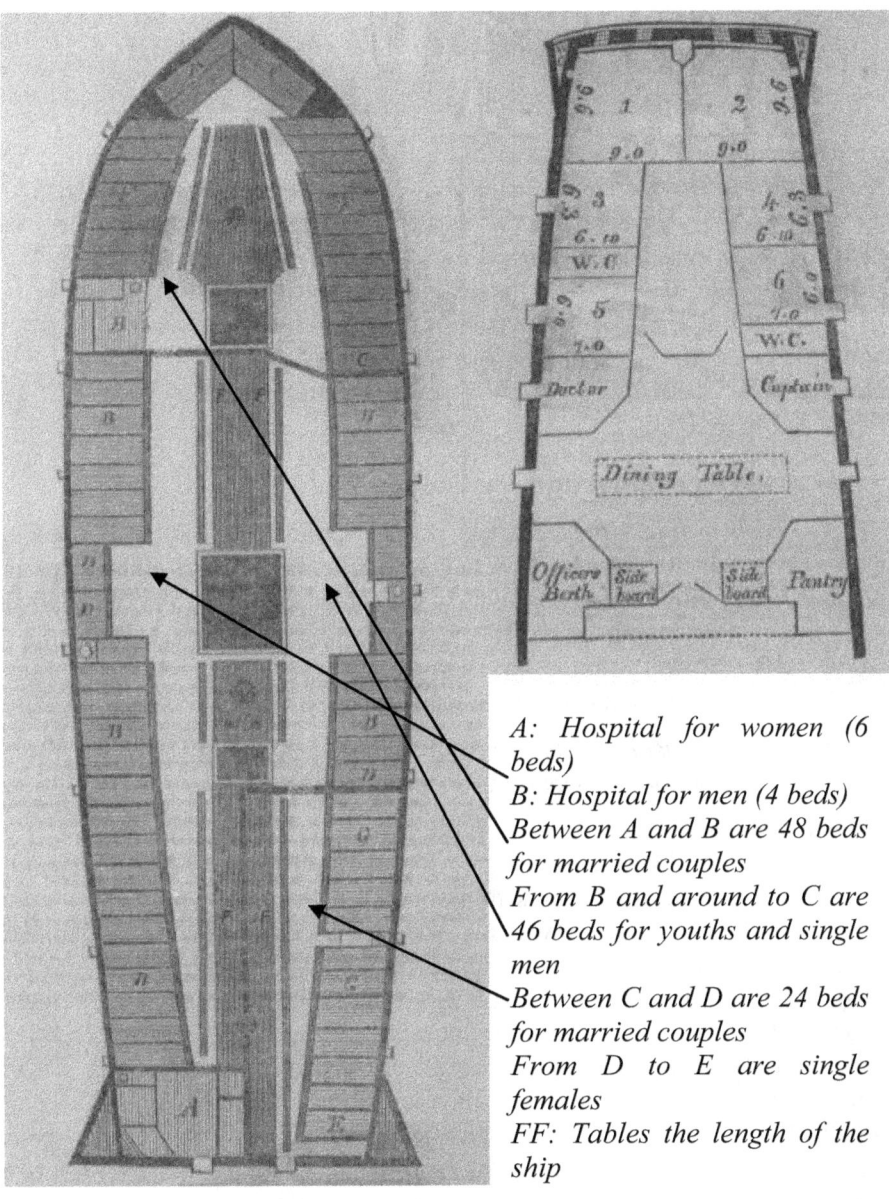

A: Hospital for women (6 beds)
B: Hospital for men (4 beds)
Between A and B are 48 beds for married couples
From B and around to C are 46 beds for youths and single men
Between C and D are 24 beds for married couples
From D to E are single females
FF: Tables the length of the ship

Plan of Emigrant Ship Between Decks (left) and Plan of Cabin Accommodation (right) (courtesy London Illustrated News)

Wars and the *Lancashire Witch*

The *Lancashire Witch* and the Crimean War

The *Lancashire Witch* was listed with many other ships as being used for the Transport Service for the British Navy and Army, on 1 May 1855.[25] The *Lancashire Witch* arrived at Spithead, Hampshire, England[26] to pick up 130 fine young horses and 60 men of the 1st Royal Dragoons, and 12 men of the 10th Hussars[27] for the Crimean War.[28] They then embarked more cavalry at Portsmouth consisting of Cornet G. S. Davies, 1 sergeant and 50 men of the 10th Hussars, from the cavalry depot at Maidstone. The Hussars were from India. They were to be remounted on arrival in the Crimea,[29] specifically Balaklava.[30]

The *Lancashire Witch* and the Second Opium War

The *Lancashire Witch* played a key part in another war called the Second Opium War which ran from 1856 to 1860. The main reason for the Opium wars was the Chinese wanting to stop the spread of opium as it was highly addictive to their people. The British however were gaining a lot of money from the trade and wanted to keep it going. There were also other conflicting views which caused the wars.[31]

In 1857 the *Lancashire Witch* sailed from Hong Kong to Canton with the 59th Regiment onboard, preparared for battle.

The soldiers had a drinking session the night before embarking, drinking to a speedy return, "covered with glory." They all boarded the *Lancashire Witch* and because of the quick thinking of Col. Graham who put a stop to the drinking early on, there was not one drunk soldier on board. The men didn't mind that the Colonel had interfered and gave "hearty cheers" as the boats left the shore. They were on three large Chinese sampans and had a quarter of a mile march from the barrack square. The *Lancashire Witch* was moored 400 yards from the shore and the men had to go out to her on a boat and ascend the side of the ship separately. They did this extremely quickly. As they marched to where they were leaving, nearly every European in Hong Kong turned out to farewell them and there were many cheers. The regiment had been there for eight years and were well known.[32]

They left Canton on 19 December 1857 with "a bright sun," and to the tune of "God save the Queen." General Straubenzee was in the British steamer *Inflexible* with Colonel Foley, Colonel Stephenson, Captain Pellew, Dr. Dickson, and Deputy Acting Commissary-General Servantes as well as 309 Chinese Coolies and 46 Europeans of the Acting Military Train with interpreters and servants. The *Inflexible* towed the *Lancashire Witch* and there was the *Sampson* towing the *Mooresfort*.[33]

As the *Lancashire Witch* moved out of the harbour a small vessel with two Chinese women on it approached the ship. A Chinese lady held a container of crackers above her head, held up in honour of one man on board. Many people were amused by this but others realised her grief at the solider leaving her.[32]

The *Lancashire Witch* had on board Colonel Hope Graham with 400 rank and file of his 59ths and also 300 Chinese of the Military Train.[33]

The *Sampson* had Dr. Gordon, commissariat and medical officers and 200 Coolies, as well as money for the troops.[33]

On the *Mooresfort* were three batteries of the Royal Artillery under Capt. Rotton with lots of ammunition and stores.[33]

A Chinese Coolie was generally a slave or worker hired at a cheap rate.[34] The Coolies were enlisted with the British Military and received clothes, bedding, rations and seven dollars a month each. They wore black jackets with a white stripe from the left shoulder to the right hip. They were numbered in Chinese and English on the back and front and wore a bamboo cap painted red.[33]

They reached Deep Bay and saw the walled city of Namtow. By the time the *Lancashire Witch* and *Inflexible* reached the Bogue (a narrow strait in the Pearl River Delta, Guangdong, China), it was dusk and the tide was wrong. During the night a little trading steamer supplied the fleet.[33]

It was 4 pm on Sunday before the *Inflexible* cast off the *Lancashire Witch* at the bottom of the Reach of Bamboo Town.[33] At one stage during this journey the *Lancashire Witch* got aground in the mud which delayed them for two hours. The Rev. Mr. Huleatt read prayers to the troops while they waited. At their mooring they were 12 miles now from Canton.[32]

On Monday 28 December 1857 at 6am the bombardment of Canton commenced. The Chinese would have been very scared as there was "incessant discharge of shot and shell from guns and mortars of immense calibre." The land forces consisting of the 59th (which had been transported on the *Lancashire Witch*) as well as many others, landed and advanced eastward against the Tung Pautoi.[33]

After transporting the troops into battle, the *Lancashire Witch* stayed in the Canton Harbour as a hospital ship for a long time. It was being hired at 18s per ton per month and had never had more than 140 people on board. This was costing £10,000 for about 120 men for nine months, which was seen as exorbitant and laughable.[35]

In March 1859, it was noted that the *Lancashire Witch* was sailing back to London with 5000 bales of hemp on board. This shipment would give the owners a good profit.[36] On 25 October 1859 the ship left London with Captain A. Molison at the helm, arriving in Bombay, India. On board were 214 soldiers, wives, 239 children and 10 married couples, and six single men with surgeon being Dr. Anderson.[37]

The *Lancashire Witch* then went back to being a hospital ship in Hong Kong with Captain Molison in charge.[38] Of the four hospital ships stationed in Hong Kong, (including the *Mauritius*, *Melbourne*, *Sir William Peel* and the *Lancashire Witch*), the *Lancashire Witch* was described as the "crème de la crème." The ship was fitted out in Hong Kong with iron beds riveted tight to the deck. The wards were well ventilated and even early in the morning they smelt fresh with no bad smells. There was no engine-room to break the sweep of the deck, as in the steamers, so "the most perfect ventilation" was obtained.

The *Lancashire Witch* had two officers and 82 men on board with accommodation for up to 96. The men wore flannel clothing with a clean pair of sheets and "famous blanket." There were lots of books and London papers for them to read which the men were very grateful for.[39] Many sick men would have passed through the ship, being tended for wounds and other illnesses.

The capture of Yeh after the fall of Canton (Creative Commons Attribution Licence 3.0)

Captain Molison and His Wife

Captain Alexander S. Molison apparently sailed the *Westminster* to the Bay of Islands, New Zealand in 1840. He then sailed to New Zealand with troops on board in 1856. He was also the Captain when the *Lancashire Witch* sailed to Canton, China in 1857. It seems his wife was pregnant during this journey and probably sailed on board with him. While the *Lancashire Witch* was sitting as a hospital ship he took up a job to sail the *Hougoumont* from Hong Kong to Sydney and on this journey his second son William. J. Molison was born on 11 February 1858, while at sea.[40]

What an adventurous life for the wife of a sea captain!

An Abandoned Trip?

The *Lancashire Witch* (1386 tons) was advertised as travelling from Plymouth to Sydney with immigrants, leaving between 27 March and 4 April 1862. The charge for an adult being £14 2s 6d.[41] This trip however never took place. Instead she came to Lyttelton, New Zealand the following year.

Deck of an emigrant ship (Artemisia), The Illustrated London News, 12 August 1848.

The Final Years of the *Lancashire Witch*

In 1877, it was reported in newspapers that the *Lancashire Witch* was caught in an "earthquake wave." According to reports the ship was completely destroyed. The tsunami was caused by the Iquique earthquake of 9 May 1877, an earthquake estimated to be at 9 magnitude.[42] Seventeen ships were lost on the Peruvian coast. Fifteen of the ships that were lost were loaded with guano and the other two probably loaded with guano also. The guano trade was a huge business at this time, with the loads being used for fertiliser around the world. There was no news of what happened to the crews of the ships.[43]

This report appeared to be the end for the *Lancashire Witch*, however, it appeared that ship was not fully destroyed as first stated. It is listed the next year in the Lloyd's Register of Ships and was still a working ship, owned by H. Fernie and sons and registered at Liverpool. It then changed owners a couple of times, but was still registered in Liverpool for about a year.

In 1878, the ship was registered at Lima, Peru to Grace Brothers. It was still rigged as a clipper ship but was no longer British owned.

By the 20th century the *Lancashire Witch* was getting fairly old for a wooden clipper ship. It was still registered in Lima in 1900. A record of what finally happened to it cannot be found. It is likely it was just left to rot somewhere near Peru, or maybe it had an accident or was used for scrap, but we don't know for sure. Whatever happened to the *Lancashire Witch*, it had a good innings for a wooden clipper, and many adventurous journeys around the world.

Lima Harbour, Peru, 1860s (Creative Commons Attribution Licence 3.0)

Lancashire Witch Advertisements

> CANTERBURY, New Zealand.—The PASSENGERS' LINE.—Under special engagement with the Provincial Government to sail June 18, the splendid liner LANCASHIRE WITCH, A 1, 1,750 tons register; in the East India Docks. This ship has been almost entirely rebuilt, and specially adapted for the passenger trade, with the object of incorporating every recent improvement of modern ingenuity.—She has been subject to the closest inspection by the most celebrated surveyors in London and Liverpool, and universally admitted to be in strength and symmetry a perfect merchant ship. From her great size, her accommodation is much above the average in comfort, and she will be fitted with a full size distilling apparatus, making upwards of 500 gallons of pure water daily. Passengers by her will secure an amount of comfort almost unknown hitherto in the New Zealand trade. Before her present improvements were undertaken she was noted as the fastest clipper in the fleet of the late Duncan Dunbar, Esq., having made the voyage to Auckland in the shortest period ever known. She may now be expected to eclipse her past reputation, and shippers may therefore calculate on having their goods delivered in a shorter period than has ever yet been accomplished. Apply to Seymour, Peacock, and Co., Fenchurch-street; or to Shaw, Savill, and Co., 34, Leadenhall-street, London, E.C.

The Times (London) 22 May 1863

> NEW ZEALAND.—The PASSENGERS' LINE.—Assisted and free passages.
>
> | Ships. | Tons. | Port. | To Sail. |
> |---|---|---|---|
> | Greyhound | 3,600 | Canterbury | Jan. 16 |
> | Canterbury | 3,000 | Ditto | Feb. 10 |
> | Winterthur | 1,500 | Auckland | Jan. 14 |
> | Lancashire Witch | 3,000 | Ditto | Jan. 25 |
> | Ulcoats | 1,500 | Ditto | Feb. 10 |
> | Lizzie Southard | 2,000 | Otago | Jan. 23 |
> | John Duncan | 2,000 | Ditto | Feb. 15 |
> | William Gynther | 1,000 | Nelson and Napier | Jan. 30 |
> | Berar | 2,000 | Wellington | Jan. 25 |
> | Martin Luther | 1,500 | Wellington and Taranaki | Feb. 15 |
>
> The abovenamed ships, with others equally magnificent to follow, constitute a passenger fleet worthy of inspection by all interested inquirers. They are all first-rate passenger packets, fitted and equipped upon plans founded upon long experience. Intending emigrants will find them perfect in the most minute details.—Shaw, Savill, and Co., 34, Leadenhall-street, London.
>
> AUCKLAND, New Zealand.—Free and assisted passages and free grants of land.—First ship, now fast filling in the East India Docks, the well-known first-class clipper WINTERTHUR, 1,500 tons, WILLIAM GOUDIE, Commander. The accommodation for passengers in this vessel has just been entirely remodelled, and is now unexceptionable. Immediate application should be made for her two disengaged poop cabins. She will be followed by the unrivalled clipper ship.
> LANCASHIRE WITCH, A 1, 3,000 tons, noted for her great strength and speed, and sound delivery of cargo. The beautiful new clipper
> ULCOATS, A 1 12 years, 1,500 tons, will be the succeeding packet. This fine vessel has just returned from her first voyage to New Zealand, and offers an excellent opportunity for all classes of passengers.
> Full particulars as to the condition on which free grants of land and free and assisted passages by these ships are granted will be obtained on application to Shaw, Savill, and Co., 34, Leadenhall-street, London, E.C.
>
> LANCASHIRE WITCH for AUCKLAND.—Shippers are requested to forward their goods intended for this favourite vessel to the East India Docks without delay.—Shaw, Savill, and Co., 34, Leadenhall-street, E.C.
>
> AUCKLAND, New Zealand.—Free Grants of Land

The Times (London) 14 January 1867

Voyage to Wellington & Auckland
(4 April 1856 – 20 July 1856)

Voyage to Wellington & Auckland, 1856

The first New Zealand voyage of the *Lancashire Witch* happened in 1856, when she was barely two years old. She left Gravesend on 4 April 1856[44] and Portsmouth on 17 April 1856[45] with Captain A. S. Molison at the helm. It was listed as a ship of 1386 tons and was being used by the British Transport Service as a transport for British troops.

It was a fast and easy voyage, but there were four deaths on board, two of those being children. There were also two births. On 25 May, in latitude 29 degrees 27 minutes south, longitude 23 degrees 55 minutes west, Ensign Lewis Harrison of the 11th Regiment accidentally fell over board from the poop and was drowned. The seas were very high and tragically there was no way the crew could assist him.

They spoke only one vessel on the voyage, the Ellen Bates on 22 June at 43.93 S, 106 W. She was 75 days out from Liverpool, bound for Melbourne.[46]

After 77 days travel they stopped at Hobart to unload a portion of the 12th regiment (855 men)[47] and then went on to Sydney. They landed a detachment of the 11th regiment (5 officers and 72 men)[47] at Sydney. There were 257 men on board from the 65th regiment under the command of Captain Peebles of the 11th regiment. Also on board were Ensigns Lewis, Leonard and Pennefather of the 65th regiment and Assistant Surgeon Birkett of the 74th regiment.[48]

It took only 8 days to travel from Sydney to Wellington which was a very quick passage. She was one of the largest ships to have entered Wellington harbour. The total journey between Portsmouth and New Zealand was 92 days, very rapid considering there were two stops on the way.[48] The *Lancashire Witch* brought mail to New Zealand from the colony and European newspapers from 27 March to 17 April.[49]

It arrived at Wellington on Sunday 20 July dropping off 3 officers and 251 men[47] of the 65th regiment, and departed on Monday 28 July for Auckland via Cape Palliser which is a cape at the bottom of the North Island. The ship travelled up the east coast of the North Island for Auckland. It arrived off Cape Colville and sailed into the harbour before noon on Friday 1 August 1856.

The ship brought to Auckland a small detachment of the 65th regiment which included Captain Blewitt, 28 soldiers, 7 women and 8 children. Captain Peebles of the 11th regiment was on board as well as Assistant Surgeon Burkitt of the 74th regiment and one private of the Royal Sappers and Miners.

The papers commented that the *Lancashire Witch* was the largest ship ever to have entered the harbour at Auckland and was called "a magnificent specimen of marine architecture." Captain Molison had sailed the ship *Westminster* to the Bay of Islands in March 1840 so was known by some in the area. The *Lancashire Witch* was the property of Captain Molison and Messrs. Duncan Dunbar and Son.

The *Lancashire Witch*, for Shanghai,[50] left the port of Auckland just before noon on Friday 8 August, and finally left the North Head on the morning of Saturday 9 August 1856.[51]

Two ships, the *Ashmore* and the *Lancashire Witch*, both from the port of Auckland, arrived in Hong Kong on the 20th and 23rd of October 1856, respectively.[52]

The fast passage of the *Lancashire Witch* was still being talked about in 1862 with the 105 day passage from Portsmouth to Auckland (with three stops) not being repeated.[53]

The 65th regiment was involved in the Taranaki Wars of 1860 to 1861 and the Waikato War of 1863 to 1865. They were known to the Maori as the "Hickety Pips" due to the Maori pronunciation of the number 65.[54]

THE clipper ship
'LANCASHIRE WITCH,'
1386 tons register, ALEX. L. MOLISON, Esq., commander, will sail as above on Thursday, 7th instant.
For passage (being an eligible opportunity for passengers to England by the overland route.)
Apply to
JOHN SALMON & Co.
Queen-street Wharf.
4th August, 1856.

Daily Southern Cross, 5 August 1856

Voyage to Wellington & Auckland 1856

Map of the Journey of the Lancashire Witch

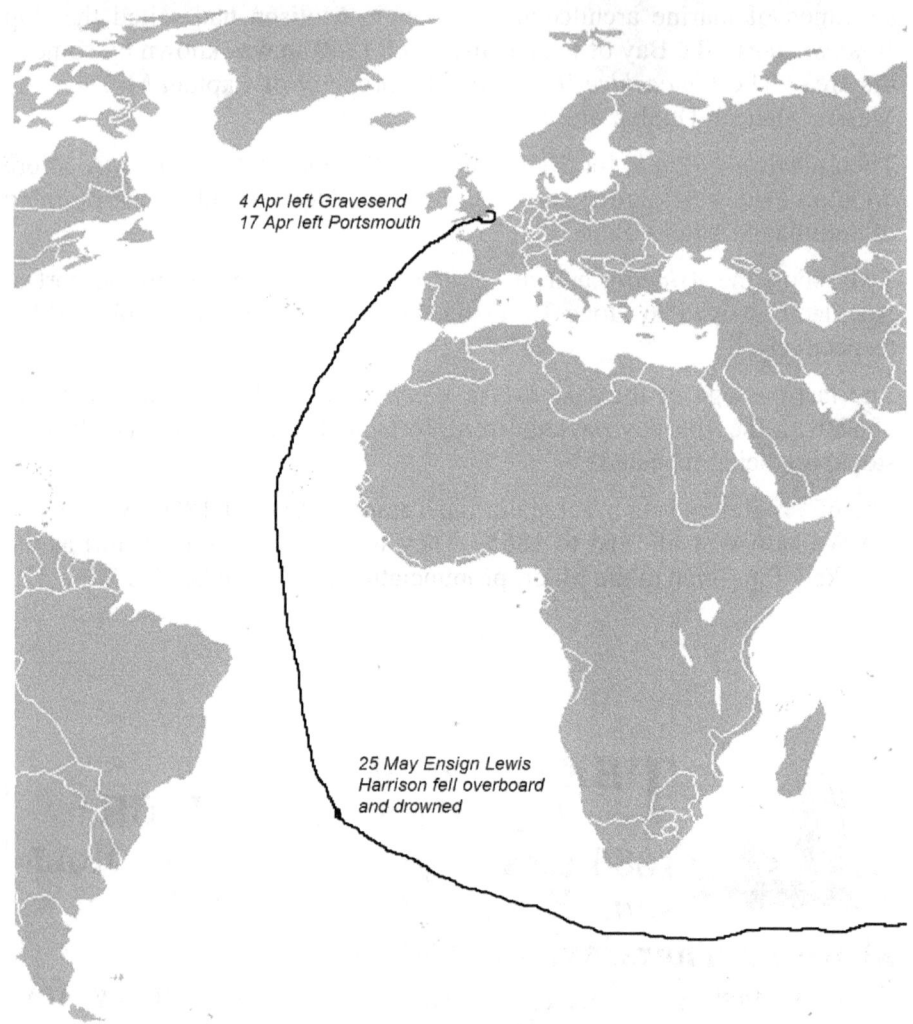

(4 April 1856 – 20 July 1856)

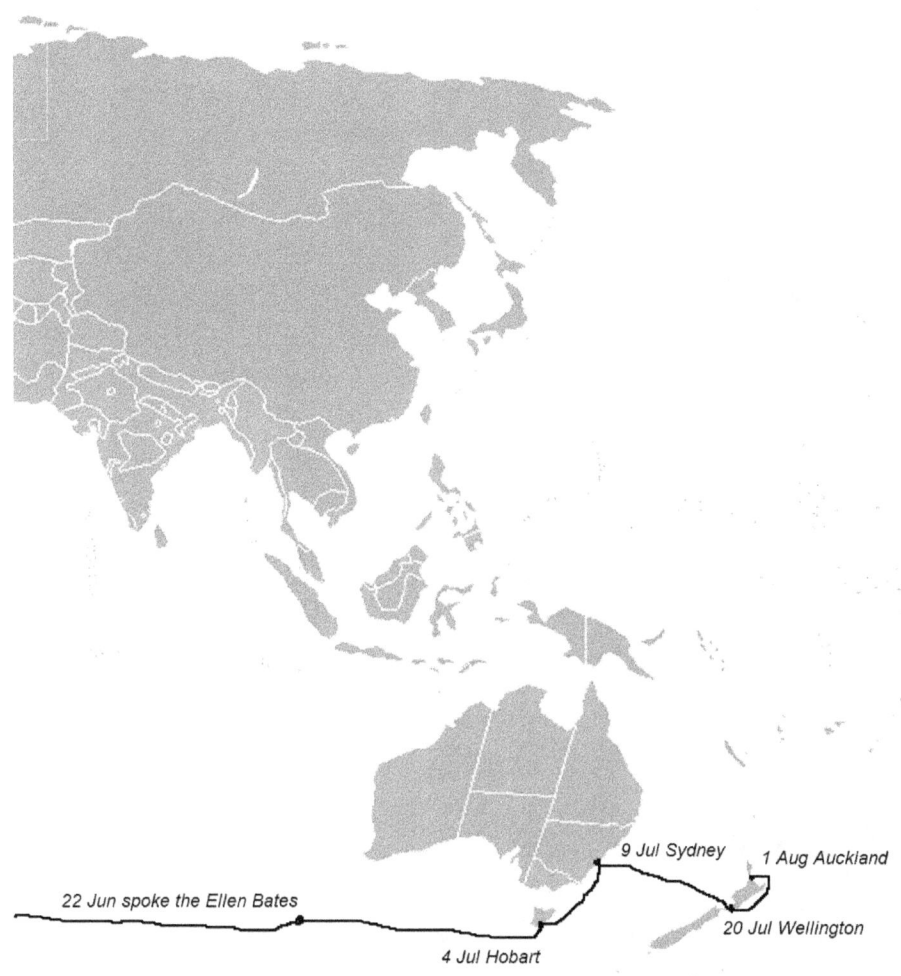

Passengers to Wellington & Auckland 1856

Passengers to Wellington & Auckland, 1856

Farmer

John Farmer was born in Bristol, England in 1839 and entered the Imperial Army in the 65th Foot in England in 1855. The next year he arrived in Wellington on the ship *Lancashire Witch*. He spent two years at Wellington and then served at the Auckland, Taranaki and Waikato campaigns against the Maori. He was discharged in 1865 and became a policeman two years later in the Hawkes Bay region. After serving in the police for 13 years in Napier, he was transferred to Poverty Bay in 1880 and became Constable in charge of the Ormond District in 1885.[55]

Goodman

Daniel Goodman was born in County Down, Ireland and enlisted in the 65th regiment. He came to Wellington, New Zealand on the *Lancashire Witch*. He was in Waitara and the Waikato District during the Maori War and received the New Zealand War medal and two conduct badges for his service.[56]

Grant

William Grant was born in India. He enlisted in the 65th regiment in 1853 and travelled to New Zealand in 1856 with his wife on the *Lancashire Witch*. He fought in the Taranaki war under Colonel Gould and then in the Waikato, where he took part in two famous fights against the Maori at Rangiriri and Orakau. He received a New Zealand war medal and the Imperial pension. He died after a short illness at his house at Cobden Street, Auckland in 1911, aged 74 years. He left an adult family of six sons and two daughters. His wife died two and a half years before him.[57]

Grey

James Grey was apparently on board the *Lancashire Witch* in 1856 according to a newspaper report. He had two aliases: Gaffney and Lee. He was originally from Ireland and a lawyer aged 43 in 1878. He was Roman Catholic and could read and write. He was brought up before the Supreme Court for forging and uttering.[58]

Harrison

Mr William Greer Harrison was one of the men in the 65th regiment. He held the position of lance-sergeant but was tried by court-martial for being drunk while on duty and he was "reduced to the ranks." A whole lot of witnesses testified that William was perfectly sober! William then set up the first temperance society in the regiment. He married the daughter of the barrack sergeant at the time and then managed to get discharged into civilian life.[59] He became a business man in Auckland. William then presented a speech for Earl Beaconsfield's services to the empire while in Californian.[60]

Heenan

Charles Heenan was born in County Down, Ireland and left for New Zealand in 1856 on the *Lancashire Witch*. He was a member of the 65th regiment. He took part in the Maori Wars in Taranaki and Waikato. In 1862 he arrived at Onehunga and married the same year. He left the army and started farming. He was of a "kindly and charitable disposition" and was very popular.

His health deteriorated and he died in his 69th year, leaving a widow and ten daughters as well as 16 grandchildren. He loved the Friendly Society and assisted in the formation of the local Hibernian Society and was the first president. The Hibernians were pall-bearers at his funeral.[61]

Hipango and Taylor

Hoani Wirimu Hipango was the leader of Ngati Tumango, of Te Ati Haunui-a-Paparangi. He was born around 1820 and married in 1841 to Rawinia Rere. They had nine children.

He was described by missionary Richard Taylor as the most influential Wanganui leader in the 1840s to 1860s. He travelled with Rev Taylor to England in 1855 and in London he met Queen Victoria and Prince Albert and presented them with gifts from the Wanganui tribes. Hipango was Christian and was shocked to see the violations of the Sabbath in London. He returned to New Zealand in 1856 on the *Lancashire Witch* with Taylor and tried unsuccessfully to mediate between warring Taranaki tribes. Hipango died in February 1865 after being wounded in a battle.[62]

Richard Taylor was born at Letwell, Yorkshire, England in 1805 and died in Wanganui in 1873.[63]

Thornton

Edward Thornton was to appear in the high court in 1874. He had come out on the *Lancashire Witch* in 1856 and was described as a 40 year old publican from Ireland. He was a Roman Catholic and was married. He was going on trial for attempting to commit suicide.[64] He lived another 20 years and died in 1894.[65]

Hoani Wiremu Hipango (right), with Richard Taylor (centre) and his son Basil (left), England, 1855. Permission obtained from Alexander Turnbull Library. Reference: PAColl-5185

Voyage to Timaru & Lyttelton
(4 July 1863 – 13 October 1863)

Voyage to Timaru & Lyttelton, 1863

The *Lancashire Witch* was chartered by Shaw, Savill & Co. to deliver immigrants to Timaru and Lyttelton New Zealand. The ship *Accrington* was the ship to sail before the *Lancashire Witch*. She was described as a ship of large dimensions (1931 tons register) which would have seemed "simply ridiculous" six years earlier as it would have required twelve months work to try and load her with immigrants. In 1863 however people were starting to hear about how great New Zealand was from friends and relatives who had already come to the colony and such a ship could easily be filled. The *Lancashire Witch* was not much smaller than the *Accrington* and would have been looked at in a similar light.[66]

The *Lancashire Witch* had been entirely rebuilt and especially fitted up for the transportation of emigrants. Apparently her passenger accommodation was excellent.[67]

There were three ship diaries for the voyage to New Zealand. Arthur Price, in the second cabin, talks about his daily routines with his wife Lissy and has a tragic and heart wrenching story of a burial at sea. David Carr in steerage (single men) has a poetical way of writing that evokes the adventures of sea travel. Henry Thorne Shepherd, a cabin passenger, was concerned mainly with the Latitude and Longitude which are useful for pinpointing where people were buried at sea and where events happened. He was also excited about the visit to Cape Town and anything factual. Together, the three diaries' different viewpoints provide an amazingly full account of the 1863 voyage and give us a thorough insight into ship life.

Carr starts his diary before the other men, on 27 June, when he boards a ship that sails down the River Tay and along the coast to London, leaving his home of Leith, Edinburgh far behind. There was sickness on board the ship but not for Carr who stood on deck until the light faded and he could no longer see his Scottish home. He wondered if he would ever see this land and his friends and family again. On arrival in London he saw the *Witch* in the East India Docks and then did a tour of London over the next couple of days. On 1 July he walked around the streets near the East India Docks. His luggage went on board and he was amazed at the sight. "Bales of goods, coal provisions, trucks etc. going on board in double quick time." He got his berth number which was 53 and slept on board that night.[68]

The journey started on 2 July 1863 with the *Lancashire Witch* in the East India Docks still being loaded; the men working all through the night to get the job done.[68] The ship left the East India Docks in London and sailed to Gravesend on 2 July 1863 leaving at 11am.[68] Fellow second cabin passengers Mr and Mrs Bodger from Bedford were "very nice companions," according to Price. He had coffee for breakfast and roast beef for dinner. The passengers went ashore at Gravesend and bought a few things they needed for the journey. This was common practice.[24] There was some music and dancing on board which was enjoyed by passengers.[68]

There was a government inspection at Gravesend the next day and one family, named Felstead, was ordered to leave the ship, as their boy had whooping cough.[69] Apart from this family the ship passed the inspection. Captain West was the commander of the *Witch*. The passengers were put into groups of 6 to 11 with a head messman or Captain in charge. The Captain was responsible for getting the meat and dividing it equally between the passengers.[68]

On 4 July the ship left Gravesend at about noon and they reached the mouth of the Thames by about 5 o'clock. At 8pm they could see the cliffs of Dover and the lights of Deal where they anchored for the night. Two steam tugs left the boat.[70]

On 7 July the *Witch* encountered strong head winds and had to tack which caused the ship to lean to one side a lot. Some passengers struggled to walk and some were feeling very sick and wishing they were back on land. In the afternoon they saw the *Eddystow*.[70] The ship was travelling at about seven knots per hour. Animals sighted included a whale and lots of seagulls. Also, two butterflies came on board.

The next day was much more favourable in terms of the wind. They were opposite Landsend in the afternoon.[70] Some passengers were still very sick as the ship was rolling a lot. They were travelling at about 8 knots per hour. There was slight rain in the morning.[24] Provisions were dished out on this day.[68]

During the first week out Dr. McLean checked the medical supplies and found some items to be deficient and others absent which didn't bode well for the rest of the journey. He described having a few cases of infantile gastric remittent fever within the first week but all cases were fine. Then he had a small girl with scarlatina but she did well. A second small girl got the disease and was also okay. But after this the disease spread and was impossible to contain. Other diseases that appeared a short time after were measles and whooping cough.[69]

On 9 July the ship was sailing at about 4½ to[24] 8 knots per hour.[70] There was a bit of rain and it was cloudy and dull. Price had boiled rice, ham and a bottle of beer for dinner.[24]

The ship travelled at 14 knots during the night. They were sailing nine knots per hour on 10 July with fine weather. They passed the Bay of Biscay. The ship was still heaving but some passengers were starting to feel better.[24] Four beautiful porpoises were alongside the ship. All seemed happy on board. The sailors had a violin at the front of the ship and lots of concertinas were on board. There was dancing and singing. Some sang hymns and some other songs. A school was going to be started on Monday for the children on board.[24] Carr was baking and said he "will be a passable baker."[68]

Saturday 11 July and the ship was travelling at between 10[70] and 11 knots per hour with all the sails set.[24] The ship had rolled a lot in the night and made the timbers creak on board, and some passengers had trouble sleeping. Mr Bodger had diphtheria but was feeling better that morning. His throat had been burned by the medicine (caustic) which the Dr had administered. Lunch for Price and his wife was bread, cheese and beer.[24] They passed two or three ships and about a dozen porpoises were around the ship. "They appear like so many hares" said Carr. It was a beautiful evening[24] with amazing sheet lightning.[68]

On Sunday they had quiet time for the religious services,[70] which were taken by the schoolmaster at 11.15am as well as one in the afternoon. Many people attended.[24] Price's wife Lissy was feeling very ill but managed to eat four biscuits and drink one glass of port wine. The ship was off Lisbon and the weather was warm but the ship was travelling slowly at only 4 to[24] 6 knots, almost becalmed.[68] They were at latitude 42-32 N and 13-32 W. Dinner was soup, ham and pudding.[24]

The weather on 13 July was dull and cloudy and the ship was going very slowly at about 3 knots per hour. The sea was very smooth.[24] The *Lancashire Witch* passed another ship at 4am and left her far behind.[68] Price named his cabin "Wellhead College" and gave it a good clean by scraping it.[24] Two[70] or three[68] men climbed up the rigging and the sailors came and tied them to the mast as punishment. One however, got away. They were fined 4s each (or a bottle of whiskey each)[70] before they were freed.[68] Price had supper at 8pm and had a long walk on deck before retiring at 10.30pm.[24]

On 14 July there was a good breeze of 8 knots per hour and the ship was in the lat 38-42 North, Long 15-4. They were still opposite Lisbon.[70] Carr lost his pipe overboard while drawing a pail of water for a woman. The young woman said "It will save the tobacco," which was the only consolation. Carr had a bit of a party at night or "tripped the light fantastic," as he put it. One of the messes took away another mess's blanket which sent him searching for it. While he was searching they put it back under the man's bed. Two others found it and laughed at him.[68] Antics like this helped the passengers to get through the monotonous journey.

The next day had good weather and they were travelling 8[70] to 9 knots per hour.[24] They were near Madeira at 11 am and were hoping to see the island that day. They passed a British Man of War (name not given). They hoisted the Union Jack and the *Lancashire Witch* replied by displaying their flag from the mizzen top mast. Mr Price and Mr Sheppard had three games of chess and Mr Price won all of them. But Mr Shepherd won three games of draughts in return.[24] The young men asked permission for an hour's dancing with the single women who they were not allowed to mingle with, and the Captain allowed this, much to the joy of the single men.[68]

On 16 July the ship was heading towards the tropics with warm and fine weather and a beautiful morning.[68] They passed Madeira and were now opposite the Canary Islands at latitude 33-45 N, Long 18-32.[70] The constable Richard Pelvin, who attended the women, got into trouble by climbing the rigging and got tied up (in a spreadeagle from what is mentioned). The sailors asked passengers to free him by paying them. Nobody liked him as he reported every little thing to the Captain, so he stayed in this position for some time with people laughing at him. He agreed to pay a fine, but only had 2s so the first mate paid the other 2s so he could go free. The passengers saw fish called "pilots" swimming under the bows of the ship. It was dark at 8pm.[68]

It was again beautiful weather on 17 July with the ship travelling from 8[70] to 11 knots.[68] They were at 31-43 N, Long 21-7 West. They passed two large ships but they were too far off to speak with and the *Witch* soon left them behind. The *Lancashire Witch* was very fast.[24]

They were at 28-56 N and Long 21-7 W on 18 July and sailing at about 9 knots per hour.[70] They passed a Dutch ship named *Holland*,[24] from Bramihar[68] bound for the United States.[24] The *Witch* hoisted her red ensign and the other ship hoisted their colours. Then the *Witch* hoisted four flags, the name of their ship and they hoisted the name of theirs. The *Lancashire Witch* was hoping to hit the trade winds the next day which would take them to a speed of 14 knots per hour.[24]

On 19th July the passengers had two reasons to remember that Sunday for the rest of their lives. On the positive side they saw flying fish, something which they would probably never see again in their lives. Carr never believed they existed until he saw them for himself.[68] The other memorable moment was a little girl dying. She was 2 and a half and had gastric fever. Price's description is heartbreaking, "The Doctor thought it was just sick-up and treated it as such until today at noon and then he found out what it was, only ill four days. Seeing the mother crying, I went to the cabin door, and there was the poor little thing gasping for breath, and making a queer noise in her throat. The mother could not bear it and had to be led on deck. The father said to me she is dying. I said I hope not. Yes he said. Its eyes were set then, and I went in and for the first time in my life saw the breath depart from one whose spirit I'm sure was carried up to Heaven. She died happily, never moved." The parents blamed themselves for her death, by bringing her on the journey at sea.[24]

On 20th July was the first sea burial the *Lancashire Witch* had experienced. The little girl was sewn into a piece of sail and two large pieces of chain put at her feet to make her sink. Her body was laid on a board and covered with a Union Jack and two sailors carried her to the side of the ship and laid the end on the side of the ship. The parents and eldest daughter followed and stood behind crying. The schoolmaster read the burial service. The father had his arms around his wife and daughter and all three were crying. The cry of the mother at the moment the body fell into the water was "dreadful" according to Price.[24] Carr comments that, "At night some parties engaged in sparring and so endeth the day, beginning with a funeral and ending with a hopping - so is human life callous and indifferent (in general) of anything but what affects themselves."[68] The ship was at 28-1 N and Long 24-12 W.[70]

On 21 July the passengers arose to find another death had occurred and the funeral had already been held at 6 am[24] with the bell tolling. It was the parents' only child (William Bush aged 5 years) and this hurt them very much to lose him. The Captain ordered passengers to have all their meals on the deck as it was "very close down below."[24] In such close confines disease would travel faster and it was getting very hot as they approached the equator. The ship was at Lat 22-12 N Long 24-12 West. The sun was straight over their heads at noon, being so near to the equator.[70] They passed a barque at 4pm on the starboard side[68] but didn't speak to her.[24] Carr comments "the *Witch* is a good goer not a ship having passed us yet." Price comments on the "splendid" night and the "moon shining like silver." They were going so fast that there was white foam around the ship.[24]

On 22 July the heat was oppressive. The crew spread sails to shade the passengers from the sun. There were many flying fish and Carr describes them nicely: "how they rise at times in crowds reminding me of a flight of sparrows out of a corn field."[68] The ship was at lat 19-36 N, Long 25-8 W and they were sailing at 8 knots an hour.[70] It was very calm and they were afraid of being becalmed. The Cook and Quartermaster were fighting a lot, but the Captain decided not to put them in irons as they were both as bad as each other.[24]

The heat was very oppressive on 23 July and they were at lat 17-3 N, Long 25-33 W.[70]

It was then 24 July and another child died, (Sarah Shipley) aged 14 months of gastric fever.[24] The ship was travelling very slowly at not more than three knots per hour. They sighted a ship which had a white hull and was thought to be an African slaver. Then two more ships were sighted, about nine and ten miles away from the *Witch*. Price says "The Captain says we all must be very particular indeed for if not, while in the tropics we shall get the ship's fever, and all die like rotten sheep." The ship was at lat 15-43 N and Long 26-45 W.[70] Some passengers were preparing to spend the night on deck because of the heat and cramped conditions below decks.[68]

On Saturday 25 July the sea was very calm and the boat was doing only 2 knots per hour. The ship was basically "becalmed," meaning it wasn't really travelling much at all.[24] Or as Carr puts it, "Lying as idle as a painted ship upon a painted ocean." There was a ship behind them which was gradually approaching as the *Witch* was not moving.[68] They were at Lat 14-13 N and 26-56 W. The baby who died the day before was buried at 5am in the morning.[24] The sun set at 24 minutes past six that night.[70]

On Sunday 26 July the passengers got up to find there was no wind and a vessel seen the night before was very close to the *Witch*. The vessel was a Hamburg owned barque[70] of 26 tons burden,[24] 31 days out from Newcastle on the way to Rio de Janerio.[68] The Captain of the barque came on board the *Witch* and spent all day there, since the ships were not moving. Carr sent a letter home with the Captain of the barque. There was no morning service due to the excitement of the other ship and a service was held at night.[70] Quite a few passengers were staying on the deck that night and many slept on deck.[68] There was a gorgeous sunset and a moon that was shining and beautiful.[24] They were positioned at 14 N, 27 W.[71]

On 27 July, there were seven ships in sight, all becalmed like the *Witch*. It was so hot that the tar on the deck was boiling and the sides of the ship were so hot that you could hardly touch them.[24] Carr spotted a shark's fin in the water but it went to the stern where the passengers were not allowed to go. There was rain from 8am to 12pm but it went away again. Carr managed to find between 11 and 12 coals from the galley which caught on fire. It luckily got put out before the whole ship caught alight![68] The Captain of the other ship came on board again. Mr Shepherd, Mr Bodger, Mr Allen, Mr Price and the first mate went for a row in the boat while the Captain was having dinner. Price described it as "splendid." There was a breeze for two hours and they started travelling at five knots per hour but then it stopped and everyone was disappointed. There was a lovely sunrise[68] and a beautiful sunset with "rich and bright" colours and the clouds looked stunning.[70]

On July 28, the ship was still becalmed[24] and they had endured 8 or 9 days of hot weather.[70] They were at lat 13-41 N and Long 26-4 W. They spoke the ship *Moonlight* from Boston.[19] Black clouds came in later in the day[24] and it rained heavily in the evening[70] and at night.[68] Carr described it as "the heaviest rain that I have ever seen." Some of the passengers had a wash on deck and splashed each other with wet clothes.[68] It would have been very enjoyable as washing was a rare occurrence on long sea journeys in the 1860s. A lot of the sails were taken in due to strong squalls and the flying jib and fore-mizzen topsail were blown away. The ship started to lean to one side so that it was like "climbing up a hill" to get to the other side! Bottles and other items were flying around in the squall.[24]

The next day the ship was travelling at six knots an hour and the wind was still strong and there was still lots of rain. There was a ship going towards the United Kingdom but it was too dark to speak to her. Price's wife Lissy was very sick and with a headache.[24] They were 720 miles from the line (equator).[68]

On 30 July they were travelling at between 5 and[68] 9 knots and heading in the correct direction.[24] They were at lat 10-35 N and Long 24-38 W. Price and his wife Lissy were suffering with sore throats. The Doctor gave them a gargle and some powder. They were very sick all night and went to bed early.[24]

Not much changed the next day in terms of weather conditions and sailing speed. Price got up at 10am; much later than his usual 6am rising. His throat was so sore and he had "violent perspirations" and couldn't eat. The ship was over on one side which would have been tiring for the passengers.[24]

Price and wife Lissy were still sick on Saturday 1 August. Price describes the weather as bad with the ship "pitching very much, cups and saucers flying in all directions, and a wave broke over the front part of the ship, and took away the name on the other side of her, swilling two men on the side of the ship."[24] Shepherd describes the day as having "good weather." They spoke the *Lalyroak* from Liverpool[68] bound for Calcutta, 30 days out.[24] There was another ship which they spoke to, but it was too far away to read the name.[24] There were a number of sails in sight.[68]

One of the sailors was washed overboard on Sunday but was picked up again and was fine. Price was feeling much better and ate ham soup and carrots. They were travelling at about 6 knots per hour[24] but the ship was still experiencing adverse conditions for sailing at Lat 5-12 N.[68]

On Monday 3 August one of the passengers struck the Cook on the head with a pot (after he put a passenger's pot on the floor and the movement of the ship made it tumble over).[68] His head was bleeding very badly.[24] The man was put in irons and confined.[24]

On 4 August they were at Lat 3-2 N and Long 21-45 W.[70] The ship was travelling at about 8 knots per hour with a strong breeze still against them.[24] They were 250 miles from the equator.[24] The case of the man striking the Cook was tried by the Captain and the passenger was released and "at his duty."[68] Price had a fight with the Steward who he described as a "bad fellow" who drank all the time and used foul language.[24]

On 5th August another child died, a small boy[24] of about 3 years old.[68] They were travelling at about 7 knots[24] and the air was cooler and milder. There were lots of porpoises around the ship and one of the quartermasters tried to harpoon one, but failed.[68] This seems very cruel to most of us these days, but the boredom of the journey plus the opportunity of some food or a souvenir made people hunt any animals that came near. Back then animals were viewed in a different light. Price had meat pie and plum pudding for dinner. The ship was at Lat 1-35 N, 24-55 W.[70]

Price got up early the next day and watched the young boy get buried but very few others were up. Because the sea water was so warm, Price and his wife had a good wash and wanted to do this every morning they could. Lissy also did some washing. Often this was done after copious rain when fresh water was collected in sails and put into barrels for this purpose. Price had breakfast at 8am, potted salmon. He was surprised to even have obtained this as well as a pot of fresh herrings. They were at Lat 1 North, 25-56 W,[24] or 25-14 W depending which report you read.[19] Price had pea soup, meat pie and plum pudding for dinner which he enjoyed.[24] Neptune came on deck and hailed the passengers from the jib boom with a blazing torch. He asked questions and told he would call the next day to get some of the younger children shaved.[68]

On 7 August they crossed the line at last after a long wait at about 2am.[70] There was no "drunken revelling" by the sailors as the Captain put a stop to it saying "the latitude they were in was too dangerous."[68] The children were also very frightened of Neptune coming.[24] Carr was very disappointed.[68] Usually on immigrant ships the sailors would put tar on the faces of those to be shaved and take it off with a piece of old iron. After this they would swill the poor passenger in a sail filled with water. You could, however, get away from this if you paid for the sailors' grog.[72]

There were lots of dolphins and porpoises jumping at about 8 am. They passed the island of St Paul but did not sight it. There were quite a few birds as well.[24]

While in the tropics, Dr McLean had ordered the ladders be pulled up in the daytime so that passengers would go on board in the fresh air, hence reducing the spread of disease. He had great difficulty with getting the passengers to go on deck throughout the voyage and there were many cases of dysentery in the tropics.[69]

There were two ships in sight on 8 August with an American ship very close to the *Witch*. The wind was light and the ship had to go into a starboard tack which was uncomfortable for the passengers. Carr was reading Walter Scott poems and was so into them he forgot he was at sea![68] They were at Lat 3-39 S, Long 30-13 W.

According to Carr four children were recorded as dying but this was probably over a few days. Also one baby girl was born. They were approaching the South American coast on 9 August and the lookout told the passengers to keep a good eye out for any shallow water.[68] They were at Lat 5-58 S, Long 32-6 W about 80 miles off the coast of Brazil.[70]

They were getting very close to the coast of Brazil on 10 August and an order came to 'bout ship but the wind changed three points within an hour and the ship turned and sailed on the right tack.[68]

By 12 August the ship was at lat 13-10 S. It was quite stormy and the ship was on one side.[70] The royal jib was turning into rags in the wind. A humorous comment from Carr was that it was the beginning on the grouse shooting season back home but nothing to shoot where he was! He did, however, see a brown bird the size of a sparrow hawk.[68] Price wrote that he climbed to the top of the masthead at 180ft high. He saw two ships from up there and called it a "splendid lookout." The ship was being thrown all over the place and Price tried to put strips on the table to stop things rolling off. Cups and saucers were flying everywhere.[24]

The next day there was a birth of a little girl and nearly at the same time a child died.[68] They were at 13-37 South, Long 36-6 W.[70]

They were at lat 18-41 S Long 36-35 W on 14 August.[70] The funeral for the child who died the previous day was held in the morning. The day was squally. They spoke a barque by using signals.[68]

On 15 August they spoke to a French barque, 46 days out from Cardiff. It was called *Hester Junior* and was laden with coal. They had a good wind and were travelling at about 10 knots per hour.[24] They were at lab 22-17 S, Long 36-17 W.[70]

On 16 August there was another birth of a girl "a little *Lancashire Witch*" as Price puts it.[24] They were travelling at about 10 or 11 knots per hour and were at Lat 26-8 S, Long 35-39 W.[70] They had the usual Sunday services and passed a ship in the afternoon.[68] They tried to speak to her but could not see her colours, only her Ensign which indicated she was English. The new moon that night looked like "a ball of fire, partly covered with a plate."[24]

Overnight they made great speed and the next day they were at 29-4 S and 32-59 and[68] were travelling at 10 knots.[24] A baby boy was born today,[68] to Mrs Bodger.[24] There were many Cape pigeons flying about and some albatross.[24]

On 18 August the passengers noticed it was getting colder.[24] The passengers boxes were taken out so they could get the things they needed for the rest of the voyage.[70] Price describes it: "Such a sight I never saw. Boxes for 500 passengers, all on deck, such a turnout."[24] They were travelling at 5-8 knots per hour with a more favourable wind.[70]

The next day another child died which made six children dead so far (or 8 according to other records).[24] Carr writes poetically, "Another child is dead. Another spirit fled. Another body overboard to mingle with the dead."[68] There was a young man ill with fever.[24] They were travelling at about 10 knots per hour with a ship in sight.[24] There were lots of Cape Pigeons which were described as "pretty birds."[70] and it was getting very cold.[24]

It was quite stormy on 20 August and very hazy which continued until about 9.30pm when it cleared and the stars filled the sky.[68] They were at Lat 34-28 S, Long 21-46 W.[70]

A storm caught the *Witch* on 21 August and four sails were blown away[24] and ropes broken by the gale.[68] Carr was woken by a "heavy lurch" and imagined the ship being smashed by the waves of the storm, but it was a false alarm.[68] One can only imagine the terrors of trying to sleep during a storm in the open ocean.

Two children died on 22 August, both boys aged 2 and 5. The five year old (Alexander Patterson) was from Dundee, and was buried only one hour after he died, but when he fell over the side his body got stuck on the ropes and swung there for a while. Price says, "but what can we expect but dreadful sights at sea." There were six young men sick with "brain fever."[24] It seemed like some had not been out of bed for weeks.[68]

Today, on 23 August, the ship passed an island called Tristan da Cunha (wrongly named "Accumtra") which was part of the Ascension Islands.[70]

They could hardly see it because of the dull day. They did see plenty of seaweed floating on the water though. Carr comments that it will be another six weeks before they see New Zealand.[68] They were at Lat 36-49 S, Long 19-8 W and sailing at 8-10 knots per hour.[70] There was only one service held downstairs. It was very cold and Price had hare soup for dinner, mashed potatoes and ham. He enjoyed his dinner very much. The monotony was starting to show as Price stated, "Had a walk backward and forward."[68] This statement creates a vivid feeling of claustrophobia and boredom.

The next day on 24 August they were at lat 37-54 S Long 5-10 W and were sailing at 10-12 knots per hour with a fair wind.[70] The sun was shining but it was getting even colder. Price comments that Lissy is getting quite fat.[24] Carr made a sponge for a loaf, played a few games of draughts and started to wash a pair of drawers.[68]

There was another death on 25 August, of a little girl, who was buried at about twelve at night.[24] There were a large number of people sick on board now.[68] They were apparently at lat 40-5 S but probably more like 37 S.[70] There was a lot of water splashing over the side of the ship and people were slipping and sliding and getting wet. This made everyone laugh![70]

The next day was similar in terms of water coming over and drenching the passengers. Many of the sails were down and the top gallants were re-fed.[70]

It was decided on 27 August that the *Witch* would stop at the Cape for medical supplies[24] as they were running short.[19] So many people were sick. They passed two ships including an American ship called the *Moonlight* from Boston. They spoke to the ship and asked for medical supplies but the other ship would not answer. Price had toasted cheese for supper.[24]

On 28 August the *Witch* was at 35-37 S Long 14-14 E. The Doctor could apparently not find a medicine chest among the stores which was the reason they were going out of their way to stop at the Cape. The sailors had to haul a great iron cable chain from the hold in preparation for anchoring at Simon's Bay, South Africa.[70] They sighted land at 4pm and as it got dark they could see the lights on Cape point.[68] An albatross was caught by hook and line.[70] A little baby died today also, another tragedy.[24]

The passengers saw the Table Mountain and Lion's Rump at about 5 pm the next day.[68] They saw a revolving light on the mountain that turned around and was visible at intervals.[70]

The ship entered Simon's Bay on 30 August and the passengers were amazed at the rocky, wild and rugged mountains on either side of them. They appeared very impressive. It took all day to sail up the bay because of the light wind. A steamer came up quickly to the *Witch*. It was the American-Man-O-War called the *Vanderbilt* which was hunting Confederate ships in the area. They thought the *Lancashire Witch* was a ship of Americans,[24] and demanded to know what they wanted there. Captain West said it was none of their business. A pilot came from the shore to the *Vanderbilt* but was not wanted so went over to the *Lancashire Witch*. The *Vanderbilt* then sailed away.[68]

The very large and frightening USS Vanderbilt 1862 that interogated the Lancashire Witch. (Creative Commons Attribution licence 3.0)

According to newspaper reports the *Vanderbilt* missed catching the Confederate ship *Georgia* which left the day before it entered Simon's Bay.[19]

Another ship to enter Simon Bay while they were moored was the *H.M.S.S. Himalaya*, with troops, on 30 August. They had made the passage from Plymouth in 28 days. This was the quickest time on record! The *Himalaya* stayed a couple of days and then left for Ceylon before sailing for Auckland.[67]

Port Officers came up and enquired as to where the ship was from, about the sickness on board and how many deaths. The doctor answered that 10 children had died so far.[70] There were also upwards of 40 passengers ill at that stage.[69] The complaints were scarlet fever, measles and whooping cough[70] as well as dysentery.[69] They would not come on board but the Doctor gave them a list of medicines needed and ordered "4 or 5 sheep, a carcase of mutton, some beef, some kegs of Cape Rum" which were brought to them. Some of the third class passengers sent 19s for some fresh meat and other supplies.[70] The pilot wouldn't take any letters ashore from the passengers in case this spread disease.[24] The *Witch* anchored in Simon's Town at about 6pm. There were about eight ships anchored there including the steamer *Himalaya* from China with 1400 troops on board and 900 tons of coal.[24] The *Lancashire Witch* was asked to raise their quarantine flag and some vessels came alongside to speak to them but no one would go on board. The passengers were very upset to be so close to land but not be allowed on shore. They even heard bagpipes "warbling their notes" on shore.[68]

On 31 August the passengers got up to an amazing sight of many vessels in the bay and two quite close, a frigate and steamer. The town was a pretty sight of white flat-roofed houses. They looked through the glass to see the names and the time on the clock. Teams of oxen came into town later in the morning laden with goods. There were beautiful houses with terraces and gardens in front of them. Carr fell in love with the place and wanted to go on shore but of course he couldn't.[68] The local Doctor and Butcher came in boats to receive their money, for supplies sent to the ship. They didn't want to touch the paper it was wrapped in and threw it away. They washed the money before they put it in their pockets, hoping to avoid the diseases on board. The boat started towards the sea again. It took all day to get down the bay due to strong winds.[24]

On 1 September they were out of the sight of land and there was another birth. At midday they were at Lat 35-47 Long 19-5. There was a rare fight between two woman today.[68] The 11 people in the second class cabins were sent a piece of Cape Beef by the Captain. The cabin passengers also ordered the butcher to sell them the carcass of mutton brought on board. It weighed 41 lbs. They then sold a part of this to the intermediate passengers but the third class passengers sadly missed out.[70]

On 2 September it started out fine but then turned into a squall. The second cabin passengers were given a pumpkin which was made into a delicious pie.[24]

The night was stormy and the passengers got little sleep as the seamen were at work on board. The Royal and Top Gallant sails had to be re-fed. The mainsail and mizzensail were "clewed up" and the ship was still going at 12-13 knots with very little sail. The steward got drunk and had no breakfast ready so the Captain kicked him out of the cabin. He also "gave him a belting"[68] for hitting two little boys.[24] In the end he had to work "as a man before the mast. In fact a common tar."[68]

On 4 September there was a search for lice amongst the passengers and this search was "generally successful."[68] Miss McWelleans in the single girls' quarters tore all her clothes off in a fit of madness and had to be held down in bed. After this episiode another girl was "Frightened . . . into a fit."[24] The ship was at lat 37-39 S, Long 28-5 E.[70]

At 2 am on 5 September the first adult died on the voyage, a 30 year old man who left a ten year old son behind. He died of scarlet fever,[24] which was extremely tragic. The ship was almost becalmed[68] and was at Lat 38-7 S, Long 31-50 E.[70]

On 6 September they made little progress due to a squall. Luckily the Captain had seen it coming and got them through it. The wind however was blowing towards them so they made very little progress. They only had five sails up.[68] The ships position was lat 38-18 S, Long 33-43 E.[70]

Two children and a married woman aged about fifty died on 7 September. This was a terrible day. The death count was now up to fourteen. They were at Lat 37-31 S Long 36-30 E.[70] Carr wrote "There has been a great morning of mortality. Before I got on deck there had been two children dropped overboard and a short time after breakfast Mrs Comming [Comyns] had gone the way of all flesh leaving behind her six motherless children and husband to mourn their loss. A loss they will long deplore for how few can live without a mother's love."[68]

On 8 September the passengers had very little sleep through the night due to the ship pitching and rolling in the rough seas.[68] An albatross was caught and it measured 9 feet from wing tip to wing tip.[70] Price mentions the albatross the next day and how the head and part of the wings were preserved.[24] Collecting parts of animals as trophies or souvenirs was common at sea in those days.

On 9 September Price sums up the day poetically with, "The sea looks beautiful, like snow, and the vessel like a desolate forest. No sails up, all bare poles."[24] Mr W. Patterson lost his eldest son also this day, meaning he had now lost two children.[68] He was the seventeenth child to have died.[68]

The next day, Shepherd comments that the contrary winds they are now experiencing will add two weeks onto their voyage.[70]

There was a huge storm with thunder and lightning on 11 September. The Captain ordered the sails to be taken down. It was so dark that you couldn't see the men in the sails taking them down, except when the lightning flashes showed their outlines above.[68] Some of the passengers were fearful of the terrible weather.[24]

Another child died on 12 September but the morning was beautiful, and sky clear.[24] They were at Lat 36-54 S, Long 42-19 E.[70]

The *Witch* was at lat 38-32 S, Long 46-42 E and was travelling at 11-12 knots per hour on 13 September.[70] The Schoolmaster, Mr Allen, who acted as chaplain caught the scarlet fever and couldn't do a service, so a Primitive Methodist Local preacher took over[70] and the passengers much preferred him to Mr Allen.[68] One of the Quartermasters (Robert W. Greerson)[73] was caught drunk with a single girl and the Captain told him to leave but he wouldn't.[24] The quartermaster had his arm around her waist and refused to move.[73] A fight ensued and the Captain was struck by Greerson.[73] The Captain then ordered the Quartermaster to be put in irons and locked up in the Quarter's Room.[24] On arrival in Lyttelton Greerson was found guilty of assaulting a superior officer and was sentenced to 12 weeks imprisonment with hard labour. In his defence he said he was only with some of his friends that he had known in England before departing. And that the Captain had struck him which caused him to retaliate. However fourth officer Mr Edward Ransom claimed he never saw Captain West strike Greerson, so there was no way out for him by self defence.[73]

Another child died on 15 September and was "consigned to the deep" at 10pm.[68] They travelled 215 miles at 10 knots per hour and were at Lat 40-31 S Long 54-38 E.[68]

One child died and another was born on 16 September.[68]

The next two days the ship was travelling fast and by 18 Sep they were at lat 42-50 S and Long 59-14 E.[70]

Sickness was starting to decrease on 19 September. There was a strong wind and they only had five sails up.[68]

On 21 September a 27 year old woman named Ann Howard[24] was walking on deck on Sunday night but very suddenly had fits through the night and died at about 9am; a terribly fast and unexpected death.[68] She had come from Lancashire, leaving behind her mother and sisters, because there were too many people in the house.[24]

It had been stormy for a couple of days and on 22 September it was hailing, snowing and terribly cold. The women were frightened.[24] They were at Lat 45-24 S, Long 80-4 E. It was so rough that the butcher[68] fell down one of the hatches and got taken to the ship hospital. Price went to the hospital to help and cut the man's hair and dressed his head. Another girl cut her forehead badly.[24] There was also the death of another child.

Carr said "Death is making a fearful havoc amongst us."[68] Price mentions that sometimes the passengers can't sleep for four or five days due to the rough nights.[24]

The next day the conditions got worse with the wind increasing and the sea "running high." The ship was rolling from side to side with items banging and moving around inside the ship. A large wave came over and drenched some of the passengers.[68] Shepherd describes the scene on deck with some excitement, "When the sun shone out, it was a grand sight to see the tempestrous sea. The tops of the waves breaking, the wind blowing the foam and making it fly like white dust." and he describes the large seas further. "It was a mercy for us the wind was blowing in the right direction. When the ship pitched down before, the sea appeared a mountain in front and when she dropt [dropped] as if it would roll right over the stern I have had a wish to see a good sea up - now I have been favourably gratified."[70] Another child died taking the death toll to 23. Carr said, "Truly this is an ill-fated ship."[68]

The next two days were still quite rough. The Lat was 45-38 S, Long 100-3 E.[70] A woman gave birth to twins but one tragically died in the afternoon.[68]

On 27 September it was a cold breeze with snow at times at Lat 47-13 S, Long 111-28 E.[68]

On 29 September they were almost becalmed and there was another birth.[68]

The next day, 30 September, it was a cold and beautiful morning and then there was a shower of snow. On 2 October two little children died and one was born.[68] And on 3 October another child died.[68] On 6 October a lot of people were washing and the anchor chains were brought up and the anchor was placed over the side ready to drop.[68]

They finally sighted the Snares, some small rocky islands south of New Zealand, on 7 October and the next day they sighted the Otago coast. They had a head wind and had to tack a great deal. On the night of 8 October a female passenger named Cook had a terrible accident. She fell on the deck, as the ship was leaning over, and cut her knee from condyle to condyle.[69] On 9 October they were almost becalmed and at night could see the lights of Dunedin. On 10 October the passengers could see the snowy tops of the mountains.[68] Shepherd described the beautiful cloud that was over the show capped mountains as being "almost supernatural."[70] They were opposite Timaru and the pilot came on board at 10am. They dropped anchor at the port of Timaru.[68] There were two boys still sick, one of gastric remittent fever and the other of bronchitis, with all others convalescent.[69] On 11 October it was "all bustle and confusion" as the boxes were hauled up and passengers landed.[70]

At Lyttelton Price commented, "Lissy quite fat and saucy." He said "We have had twenty-eight deaths and twelve births. I don't suppose I have put them all down." [24] Such was the commonness of death on board this ship that it started to almost go unnoticed by the end of the voyage. Even by someone who really cared about each death and tried to record every event.

List of Births and Deaths

There were many inconsistencies between the diaries and passenger list due to passengers writing about births and deaths sometimes a few days after the event, and the fact the Doctor didn't record every birth and death. This is probably when he was extra busy with sick people and also the fact the cabin passengers were never recorded. This list is as accurate as humanly possible.

Births

09 Aug.	Unnamed girl born
13 Aug.	Daughter to David and Maria Sneddon
16 Aug.	Unnamed girl born
17 Aug.	Boy born to Mrs Bodger
31 Aug.	Daughter of Mr and Mrs Crow
16 Sep.	Daughter of Mr and Mrs Carter
16 Sep.	Son to Thomas and Susanna Mills
20 Sep.	Son to John and Margaret Henderson
26 Sep.	Twins born to unnamed mother. One died in afternoon
29 Sep.	Unnamed child born
02 Oct.	Daughter to Charles and Catherine Menzies

Deaths

Date	Name	Age
19 Jul.	Unnamed girl (cabin passenger)	
20 Jul.	William Bush *Rubeola with parotiditis*	5 years
24 Jul.	Sarah Shipley *Diarrhoea following rubeola*	1 year
05 Aug.	John Mills *Scarlatina with tonsillitis*	2 years
08 Aug.	David Patterson *Scarlatina maligna*	Infant
09 Aug.	1 unnamed child died	

Date	Name	Age	
13 Aug.	Amelia Manning	18 mths	
	Diarrhoea following rubeola		
19 Aug.	Unnamed child died		
21 Aug	Mary Elizabeth Goodman	2 years	
	Ulcerative diarrhoea following rubeola		
22 Aug.	Alexander Patterson	5 years	
	Dysentry		
22 Aug.	Unnamed boy died	2 years	
24 Aug.	Elizabeth Grice	2 years	
	Abcesses following rubeola		
28 Aug.	Sarah Higgs	2 years	
	Pneumonia accompanying rubeola		
05 Sep.	Thomas Dunkley	34 years	
	Scarlatina maligna		
07 Sep.	Rebecca Comyns	44 years	
	Angina Scarlatina		
07 Sep.	Alfred Dawson	3 years	
	Abcesses following scarlatina		
07 Sep.	Louisa S. Bennett	6 mths	
	Pertussis		
08 Sep.	Ann Mary Carter	2 years	
	Apthous ulceration following rubeola		
09 Sep.	William Patterson	9 years	
	Scarlatina maligna		
12 Sep.	Frederick Doell	Infant	
	Bronchitis following rubeola		
14 Sep.	Janet Brackenridge	4 years	
	Pertussis		
16 Sep.	Mary Ann Welges	Infant	
	Rubeola		
21 Sep.	Ann Howard	26 years	
	Epileptic convulsions		
22 Sep.	Jasper Comyns	5 years	
	Anarsarca and bronchitis following scarlatina		
23 Sep.	Marion Sutherland	7 months	
	Marasmus (malnutrition)		
02 Oct.	Elizabeth Jane Bennett	2 years	
	Marasmus (malnutrition)		
02 Oct.	Thomas Brown	5 years	
	Convulsions following scarlatina		
04 Oct.	Joseph John Rowbotham	Infant	
	Pertussis		

Testimonials

The following testimonial was presented to Doctor McLean:-

"We the undersigned passengers on board the Lancashire Witch, on our voyage from England to Canterbury, New Zealand, desire to express our sincere gratitude for the kindness and great attention received from you; although, unfortunately, we have lost a considerable number by death, yet we feel that it has not been for want of attention or medical skill. We trust you will receive the small present as a token of esteem, earnestly hoping the remainder of your life may be blessed with every success."

[Signed by all the passengers.] "[19]

Arrival of the *Lancashire Witch*

The *Lancashire Witch* was the fourth of the first four ships to bring immigrants to the Port of Timaru, South Canterbury. The other three ships in arrival order were, the *Strathallan*, *Echunga* and *Victory*. There was a Jubilee of South Canterbury held on 14 January 1909, which celebrated the arrival of these ships. The two main items on the agenda were a procession and a luncheon of old settlers who arrived on the above ships. They also included some old settlers who were born in South Canterbury before the arrival of the first ship *Strathallan*. There was also a marine fireworks display put on by the Harbour board and the ships in the port were to participate.[74]

On the day in 1863 when the *Lancashire Witch* arrived, all those years earlier, a pilot named Mr Strong Morrison, went out on a pilot boat and boarded the ship outside Timaru, sailing it into port[75] on 10 October.[76] They landed between 100[76] and 103 passengers.[77] The immigration report stated it was 150 passengers that landed with many travelling over land to get to Christchurch.[78] On arrival the ship was checked over by Dr. Levi, the Resident Magistrate and Dr Butler. The last case of illness was only six days old but these men obviously thought most of the passengers would be well enough to land. A small boy was the sickest of all and still recovering from fever so the men decided he must stay on board. They probably should have put the ship into quarantine instead as they were not able to detain just one passenger without the quarantine label over it. Captain West was very keen to get rid of this passenger and told the Resident Magistrate that he would put the ship into quarantine himself and therefore detain everyone on board. There was a debate and eventually the child was landed.[79]

With the arrival of the *Victory* as well there were a total of about 220 passengers just landed in Timaru.[80] The new immigrants made the town have a "lively appearance." They were all settled in the barracks or tents next door and were quite content despite the fairly rudimental arrangements.[80]

While in Timaru a sailor by the name of James Creed, decided to desert. He then proceeded to steal a Police manual from the house of Joseph Lean of the Nugget Hotel. He was charged with stealing and desertion and put in prison for seven days. He was remanded to Lyttelton for the charge of desertion.[81] Maybe he had had enough of the sea and the wonderful mountains in the distance, the Southern Alps, were calling to him!

The ship sailed on 12 October for Lyttelton, arriving the next day. The newspapers printed that the diseases on board had been scarlatina, measles, and whooping-cough.[82] Three adults and 23 children had died on the voyage according to the papers, but this was a mistake. The ship arrived off the quarantine ground in Lyttelton Harbour on 13 October, making the total journey 96 days. No sickness remained on board.[76]

Quarantine Fiasco

The Immigration Commissioners report at Timaru stated that the ship was very clean and "well arranged." This was probably before the immigrants left in haste and left a mess behind them.

> **REPORT**
> OF
> **IMMIGRATION COMMISSIONERS.**
>
> SHIP LANCASHIRE WITCH.
>
> Timaru, October 16, 1863.
>
> SIR—We have the honor to report that on the arrival at Timaru of the ship Lancashire Witch, with immigrants, on Saturday, the 10th instant, we proceeded on board to inspect her.
>
> We found her clean, and everything well arranged. The immigrants were generally healthy, although there had been a great deal of sickness during the early part of the voyage, and several deaths.
>
> Under the circumstances we consider that everything was done satisfactorily, and we heard of no complaints.
>
> We have the honor to be,
> Sir,
> Your obedient servants,
> B. WOOLCOMBE,
> E. BUTLER,
> Immigration Commissioners.
> To the Provincial Secretary,
> Christchurch.

Press, 22 October 1863

After the Immigration Officers checked the ship at Lyttelton they found the ship was not in a clean condition.[78] The surgeon McLean wrote to the newspaper saying that there was a lot of packing going on at Timaru and that the passengers had left the 'tween decks in a bad state and that it was nothing to do with the state of the ship while at sea.[83] However, in the report it was stated that there was "a great accumulation of filth" under the berths, except in the single women's quarters.[78] This would have not been through immigrants packing.

The Immigration Commissioners were also not happy with the way the single women were berthed, "6 berths (2 double and 2 single berths) in enclosed cabins 6f x 6ft x 7ft." Why they were not happy was not stated. The single men were on the lower deck and had their boxes under their berths which didn't allow for cleaning.[78]

The tables were made fixtures, where they considered movable tables that could be lifted out of the way to be more "condusive to the health and comfort of the Immigrants."[78]

The Graveley's distilling apparatus had worked well, producing 500 gallons of fresh drinking water per diem over 16 working hours.[78]

Because of the illnesses, ship was to be sent to quarantine. William Donald the Resident Magistrate of Lyttelton was going to check on the buildings and surrounding land at the quarantine area when he slipped after getting out of the Harbourmaster's boat, onto some slippery rocks. He bruised his leg very badly, which got inflamed, and he ended up with erysipelas (a streptococcus bacterial infection of the skin).[84] He was seriously ill and couldn't do any of his duties.[85]

The passengers were going to be landed at Camp Bay on 13 October but the recently erected huts there were deemed unfit for habitation, so the passengers of the *Lancashire Witch* had to stay onboard. The report stated "that no man with a regard for his horse would think of using them [Camp Bay buildings] for stables." This predicament, coupled with Mr Donald's accident meant the passengers had to stay onboard until 17 October[86] a period of four days.[87] Other reports mention at least ten days detainment.[67] The newspapers commented that "The indifference of the authorities amounts almost to cruelty, when it is remembered how ardent are the longings of every landsman to get on shore after a three months' voyage."[86]

The above reports were from the newspapers but Henry Thorne Shepherd has a different story. He outlines the ship coming into the Port of Lyttelton at 11am. He calls it a "capital bay, 5 miles long by 1 broad with hills on both sides gently sloped down to the water's edge, looking green except where the rock jilted out. Mr Pain of Christchurch came on board for three sisters and a brother-in-law Mr Allan, with whom we were intimate on board. Henry went to Christchurch with him and took lodgings at the same place as W. Allan, the aforesaid schoolmaster on board. He is a painter and grainer by trade and doing well here. In the afternoon the rest of us went on shore at Lyttleton - slept there the night. The next morning we walked about Lyttleton. It is on the side of a hill. It is a very improving place and it will be a nice town. Sent some parcels by carrier. We left about 11 o'clock and found it a long and tiresome walk up the Port Hill being a warm day and we were under the wind when we got to the top and going down the other side we had rather too much wind, felt a little chilly. When we came to the bottom of the hill we got into a homnibus crossed the Heathcote River in a punt, that is a kind of floating bridge. The horses and buss [bus] were driven on, a bar put in front to keep the horses and then moved across. Came to Christchurch in time for tea."

This story totally contradicts that of the newspaper reports, the only possible answer being that some of the cabin passengers were allowed on shore while the government immigrants in steerage had to stay on board. There was also a letter written by Immigration Officer Alexander Back, describing how an immigrant Thomas Mills was allowed to land on shore contrary to Health regulations. The letter was dated 17 October 1863. It was suggested that the Captain and Surgeon allowed this and that the case should be looked into. If there was found to be a problem then gratuities paid to them would be withheld.[88] Maybe there were a couple of passengers who went ashore when they shouldn't have?

David Carr who was in steerage in the single men's compartment had a similar story to the newspapers.

Carr describes what happened on 14 October: "This morning there is no appearance of passengers being landed. A good number came from the shore to take away their friends but no brother, sister or friend came to us. Nevertheless we keep up the spirit and waited patiently to know the result of the consultation of the Authority has concerning us. The Captain came on board in the evening and said the single men were able to be landed at Port Lyttleton and to make haste as there was a fine dinner waiting for us and to take nothing with us as everything was alright. Believing his word another 14 and I got in the boat but what was our surprise when instead of taking us to the Port they landed us at the Quarantine Barracks at the opposite side of the Bay. We went up to the house but instead of a fine dinner nothing but empty houses. Some of my ship-mates looked downhearted at the prospect presented to our view. As for myself I was angry at being done in in the manner described and to be laughed at by the rest on board who would show scorn when they saw where we went. But though there was no supper awaiting us and but a hard floor for a bed, a number of us started for the top to see about us and give our limbs some exercise. After many a rest we at length got to the top and got a view of the plains of Canterbury and notably Lyttleton. We returned down the hill tired and hungry. We got a supper from some working men and one of them having a fiddle, we forgot our fortune and tripped the light fantastic toe. So with singing and dance the night passed until 10 o'clock when we sought the soft side of board and lay down to sleep."

David Carr was one of the 15 passengers who finally went on shore at Camp Bay, on 14 October after the ship was admitted to pratique (a licence to enter port after infection illness on board), but as he mentioned the passengers found the quarantine camp empty with no person to show them around and no provisions of food. These passengers eventually found their way to Rhodes Bay (now Purau) where they arrived on 23 October 1863, absolutely starving.

The passengers were very upset at the delay in getting ashore. They were still sitting off the quarantine ground on 24 October and no arrangements had been made for landing them at Lyttelton or bringing them around to Christchurch on a steamer (other reports say they were only waiting for four days). They now refused to land in Camp Bay because of what had happened.[67]

After the passengers were officially landed the newspapers discussed how badly handled the case was. The public were worried because there was talk that new cases of scarlet fever and whooping cough broke out before landing and these could be spread through town. Why was the quarantine ground not used? What was the use of Camp Bay? It had expensive "tumble-down" buildings. Why wasn't the Health Officer doing his job?[79] No one seemed to be in responsible for what had happened. It seemed that the men back in England were loading up ships for New Zealand with not much thought as to what would happen when they got there and a better system needed to be put in place. The *Lancashire Witch* was a victim of an unorganised Provincial Government.[87]

On 31 October 1863 it was noted that the Lunatic Asylum had been completed and that soon the 8 female and 14 male patients that were held in the jail and Christchurch Hospital, would be moved to their new surroundings. It was also noted that their latest patient was a young woman from the *Lancashire Witch* who had been admitted to the Asylum.[89] Maybe the long journey and the delay in landing had been too much for her?

Voyage to Timaru & Lyttelton 1863

Emigrant ship, between decks. (London Illustrated News, 17 August 1850)

What often happens when "crossing the line." The Graphic. 5 March 1881

Voyage to Timaru & Lyttelton 1863

Map of the Journey of the *Lancashire Witch*

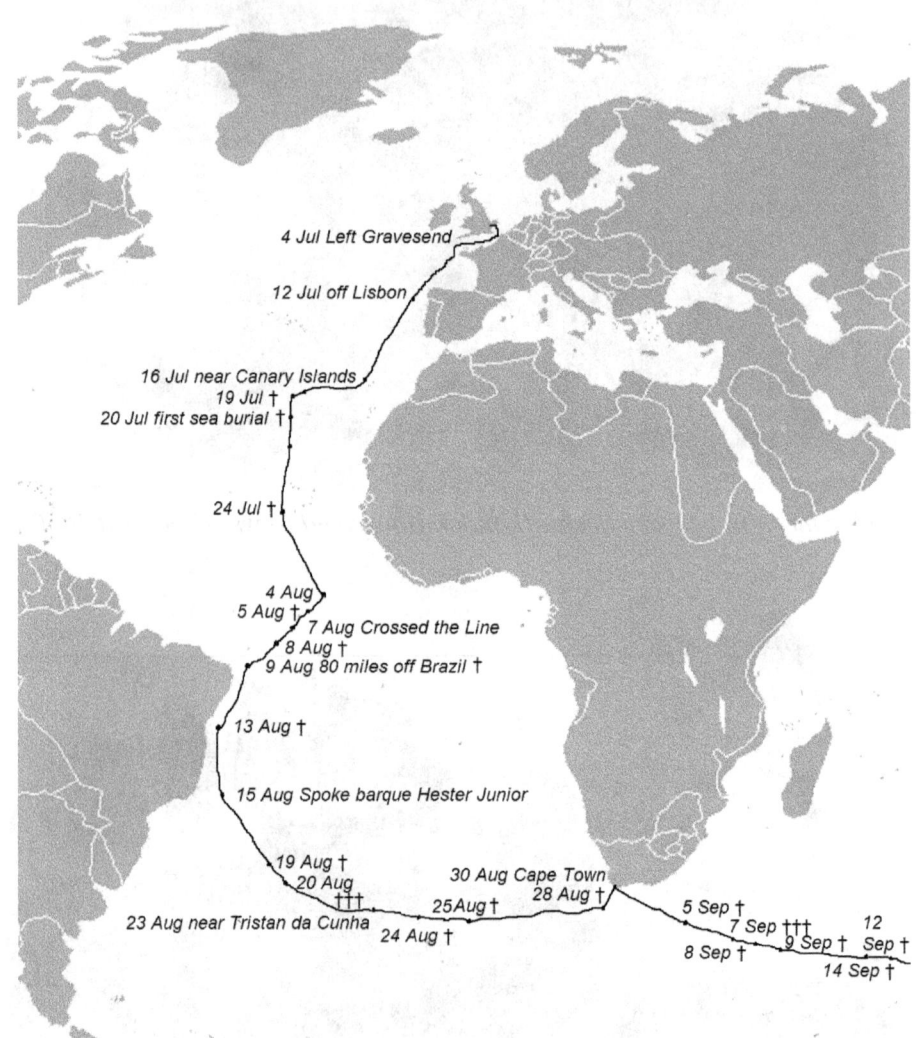

(4 July 1863 – 13 October 1863)

Dr McLean

Dr Duncan McLean came out as Surgeon Superintendent on *the Lancashire Witch*. He had also acted as surgeon on a trip out on the *Echunga* in December 1862. Dr McLean died on 11 September 1871 in Timaru. He had lived there since 1863 after arriving on the *Lancashire Witch* and was only 31 years old with a wife and young family of four.

In his obituary it is claimed that the scarlet fever on board the ship was of a virulent form and that at one time there were 250 sick people on board. He was the only doctor. Medicines ran short and he was extremely busy. A passenger gave a testimonial of his amazing service on the ship:

> "By day and by night Dr McLean was unremitting in his attention, and doing all one man could possibly do to stem the fatal tide of disease which was sweeping over the vessel. To the children especially he was most kind, and many a young life was saved by his thoughtful and persevering care. Frequently he supplied them with delicacies out of private means, which otherwise were not procurable, and even his own meals he has been known to give away to nourish some sick child."

He was just a wonderful doctor and extremely patient and kind. His funeral was a big one and the businesses of Timaru closed as a mark of respect for him.[22]

The Departure of the *Lancashire Witch*

It was thought that the *Lancashire Witch* might be placed on the berth for London to load with wool, but there is no other mention of this happening.[90] She departed Lyttelton on 5 December 1863 for Guam with Captain West still at the helm.[3]

Lancashire Witch Reunion

There was a reunion held on 17 October 1913 for the arrival of the *Lancashire Witch* in 1863. It was arranged by Mr H. Holland who was Mayor of Christchurch at the time, and Mr. G. W. Leadley of Ashburton. About 50 of the *Lancashire Witch*'s passengers were alive and most of them came to the reunion.[7] The celebrations were held at Freeman's Cafe where they had afternoon tea.

The list of those who attended were

>Mr Henry Holland (Mayor of Christchurch),
>Mr Charles Yates (Christchurch),
>Mr Richard Berry Wells (Timaru),

Mr R. Munro (Christchurch),
Mr M. Winter (Bennett's Junction),
Mrs William Elliott (Bennett's Junction),
Mrs N. Barton (formerly Miss Louisa Breessell) (Christchurch),
Mrs C. Jones (Sydenham),
Mrs J. W. Sawle (formerly Miss Jane Shepherd).
Mrs J. F. Fleming (Christchurch),
Mrs G. R. Rankin (formerly Miss Mary Draffin) (Spreydon)
Mr J. Sinclair (Christchurch),
Mrs C. Hadfield (Christchurch),
Mr G. W Leadley (Ashburton),
Mr G. W. Holland.
Mrs Giles (née Mary Ann Cass).
Mrs Fitzpatrick (née Mary Jane Leadley).
Walter Prestidge,
Jesse Prestidge,
Mrs Price,
A. H. Price,
Edward Bennett,
H. Mehrtens,
J. H. Helliwell,
Gilbert Dixon,
Thomas Arthur Dixon,
Francis Cass,
J. W. Bowman,
Adam Menzies,
Mr F. Doell (Linwood).

The following report was in the Press dated 18 October 1913:

"The party sat down to afternoon tea, and the opportunity was taken advantage of for an interchange of reminiscences.

"The Mayor, after the toast of "The King" had been honoured, read apologies from several passengers who found it impossible to be present. The apologies were from:

Mr G. W. Allen (12 Dublin Street, Christchurch),
Mr J. Robbie (Palmerston North),
Mr Thomas Prestidge (Addington),
Mrs and Miss Menzies (Opawa),
Mr J. Martin,
Mr Robert N. Adair (Bryndwr) and others."

"Mr Holland said that as one of the younger generation of those who landed by the *Lancashire Witch*, it gave him great pleasure to see so large a gathering of those who had landed in Christchurch under circumstances somewhat different from those now existing. He had been informed that the site on which the building stood in which they were assembled was brought originally at £38 per foot, and that recently £500 per foot had been refused for it. He referred to the few incidents of the voyage of the *Witch* that he could recall.

"Mr George Holland said that he had been looking forward with keen pleasure to the day's function. He could remember coming from Lyttelton to the ferry in a little steamer. At the time when the *Witch* arrived he did not think that there was then a room large enough in Christchurch to hold them; and if there had been, the streets would have been left very bare. He thought that without egotism, he could claim that the passengers of the *Witch* had left their mark on the history of the Dominion. They supplied a Mayor for Christchurch and one of the passengers, the late Mr. P. Duncan had founded an agricultural implement works that would do credit to a bigger country. He hoped that all present were happy and prosperous, and thought that a fitting manner in which to commemorate the anniversary of the arrival of the *Witch* was by extending a helping hand to those who had not been so fortunate or by assisting those who had suffered the recent colliery catastrophe in Wales.

"Mr G. W. Leadley, in proposing the health of "Surviving Shipmates," said that they were only a remnant seeing that the *Witch* brought 430 souls to the Dominion. The passengers by the *Witch* could claim that they had not lived and laboured in vain, but had assisted in taming the wilderness and made it bloom like the rose. He saw present Mr Prestidge whose father, Jacob Prestidge, was noteworthy for having brought the largest family to the Dominion by the *Witch*.

"The toast was heartily honoured and several of those present spoke to it.

"Mr G. Holland proposed the toast of "Departed Shipmates," which was fittingly honoured.

"Before the gathering broke up the party was photographed."[91]

Passengers to Timaru & Lyttelton
1863

Passengers to Timaru & Lyttelton, 1863

Aitken

Andrew Aitken was born in Dumbartonshire, Scotland in 1828. He was brought up in the country and married in 1857 to a daughter of Mr. R. Muirhead of Dumbartonshire. They came to Timaru on the *Lancashire Witch* in 1863 and lived for a while at Opuha station. Andrew then bought 25 acres of land at Opihi where he lived for the rest of his life. He was a member of the Opihi School Committee. They had seven sons and three daughters. Andrew died in 1893.[92]

Allan

George William Allan came to New Zealand on the *Lancashire Witch* in 1863. He had a business in Victoria Street for many years. He was a local preacher in the Methodist Church. He was an invalid for four years before his death, and died in 1914 of heart failure. He left a family of three daughters and two sons. His wife died about twelve years before him.[93]

Anderson

Andrew Anderson was born in Kirriemuir, Forfarshire, Scotland in 1837. He arrived in Lyttelton on 1863 in the *Lancashire Witch*. Andrew first worked on the railway line between the tunnel and Christchurch. He then worked for two years at the Canterbury Foundry as a hammerman. He bought a farm in Leeston which he worked for quite a few years and in 1877 he sold up and bought a larger farm of 222 acres. The land was in its natural state and he cultivated it and built a house and outbuildings. He also bought 320 acres of land in Oamaru. He was a member of the Leeston School Committee and was a director of the Central Dairy Company for more than 7 years. He married Miss Anderson of Perthshire and they had five sons and three daughters.[94]

Mr & Mrs A. Anderson

Beattie

William John Beattie was born in County Antrim, Ireland in 1835. He came to Timaru on the Lancashire Witch in 1863 and spent five years shepherding for Mr. John Hay in the Mackenzie Country. In 1865 he went to the Hokitika goldfields but after finding it over-crowded and overrated, he returned to his shepherding job. He took up 200 acres of land in Hilton in 1873. He was a member of the Hilton School Committee for 28 years and was connected with the Geraldine Presbyterian Church which he managed for several years. In 1871 he married Miss Bridget O'Shannesy of County Clare, Ireland and they had three sons and five daughters. Mrs Beattie came out on the ship "Queen of the Colonies," landing at Brisbane, Queensland in 1866 and travelled to New Zealand in 1869.[95]

Mr and Mrs Beattie

Bennett

John Bennett served in the Royal Navy in England and wore the "blue jacket." He actively served in the seas near China before travelling to New Zealand on the *Lancashire Witch* in 1863. In the Ellesmere district he started working as a builder until about seven years before his death. He had a "trivial" accident which gave him an aneurism and left him an invalid for about three years. He was lucky not to die soon after the accident! He started being able to walk again and took daily walks for the three years prior to his death. He however, caught a cold and because of the accident, got very sick and died. He was an Oddfellow and belonged to the Loyal Leeston Lodge. He was also a member of the Masonic lodge. He was a kind person and an "every day honest man." He left a widow and a grown up son and daughter when he died in 1898.[96]

Blyth

James Blyth was born near Arbroath, Forfarshire, Scotland in 1841 and died at Winton in 1892, aged 51. He came to Lyttelton on the *Lancashire Witch* in 1863. James Blyth died at Winton in 1892 in his fify-second year.

His second son Peter A. Blyth was born at Prebbleton in 1869. He was at one stage a member of the Winton Borough Council.[97]

Mr P. A. Blyth

Brasell

John Brasell was born in 1846 in Buckinghamshire, England and travelled to Timaru in 1863 on the *Lancashire Witch*. He was brought up with country life in the Timaru district and worked fencing, shearing and other country work. Eventually he settled in North Otago in 1876. He worked on the Maerewhenua estate for quite a while and then leased a section of twenty-two acres on which he built a cottage. He was also employed by Mr James Helley of Awaiti Farm. He married in 1874 to a daughter of Mr John Smith of Manawatu. Mrs Brasell died in 1887, leaving three sons.[98]

Buckingham

George Buckingham and his wife arrived at Timaru on the *Lancashire Witch* in 1863. They were considered some of the oldest residents of the town of Timaru. George's wife died in 1903[99] and George in 1906 aged 71 years old.[100]

Budd

William Budd was born in Staffordshire, England in 1843 and was brought up with farming. He travelled on the *Lancashire Witch* in 1863 to Timaru. He worked at Levels Station during the shearing seasons and in 1865 purchased a farm at Winchester. He wasn't really involved in public affairs but was very knowledgeable on the early history of Canterbury. He sold his farm in 1889 and bought another one, also in Winchester. He carried on mixed farming. His first wife, who he married in England in 1863, died, and he then married again to Miss Mills of Christchurch and they had two sons and three daughters.[101]

Butler

George Butler was born in Warwickshire, England in 1837. He was brought up to coalmining until he came to Timaru on the *Lancashire Witch* in 1863. Two weeks before travelling, he married Miss Hall of Atherstone. He bought land in Timaru and lived there for many years before moving to Pleasant Point in 1874 and working a farm of 300 acres. In Timaru he was superintendent of the Wesleyan Sunday School. He was elected chairman of the local school committee soon after settling in the district and resigned after ten years in 1888 when he had a trip back to England. He was elected to represent Pleasant Point Riding on the formation of

Mr G. Butler

the Levels County Council. He was a very energetic worker and wanted to advance the district. George and his wife had two sons and four daughters.[102]

Carey

George Thomas Carey was born in 1858 in Islington, England and came with his parents to Lyttelton in 1863. He was apprenticed in Christchurch where he worked for many years before opening his own boot and shoemaking business in St Albans. He spent four years there before taking over a business at Church Street, Kaiapoi in 1901. He was a member of the Christchurch Engineers for three years. He was also in the Trafalgar Lodge of Druids in Kaiapoi. George married in 1884 to a daughter of Mr W. Martin, of Christchurch, and they had three daughters.[103]

Cass

Mrs Cass was from York, England before travelling to New Zealand with her husband. They moved to Yorktown just out of Christchurch and then Wakanui near Ashburton, where they lived for twenty-seven years. She left a family of six, her oldest son having died three weeks before her.[104]

Collins

John Collins was born in Warwickshire, England and came to New Zealand in 1863. He was a talented horticulturalist and won many prizes at shows.[105] He was a pioneer settler of Tuakau and was on the School committee and Road Board. John died in 1922, aged 86 years, leaving nine sons and five daughters.[106]

Craig

John Craig was from Caithness, Scotland and travelled with his wife, Catherine née Henderson, on the *Lancashire Witch* in 1863. Catherine was from Sunderlandshire, Scotland.[107] He started off at Hornibrook Estate and then moved to Stony Gully where he resided until his death in 1906. Mrs Craig was very kind and helped people when they were ill. She died in 1911.[107] John Craig was a member of the Presbyterian Church in Southbridge since it opened. When he died in 1906, he left a wife, two sons, eight daughters and twenty-five grandchildren.[108]

Cronin

After his arrival on the *Lancashire Witch*, George Denis Cronin started working for Messrs Holmes and Richardson who constructed the railway to Christchurch. George worked his way up to senior railway official until he resigned due to illness. This same illness caused his death in 1899. George was a staunch Catholic and one of his sons was baptised on the opening day of the original church in Barbadoes Street. His funeral was heavily Catholic, the way he would have liked it. He left a wife, two daughters and three sons. Two of the children were born in New Zealand and all were married and living in New Zealand at the time of George's death.[109]

Dalton

Thomas Dalton was born in Keek, Yorkshire. He spent four years in Canada when he was young. He married Charlotte Allman, also born in Yorkshire, England and they came to New Zealand on the *Lancashire Witch* in 1863.

They first settled in Kaiapoi and Rangiora for many years and experienced a great many difficulties, as did many pioneers.[110] In 1876, after suffering some great losses in the Waimakariri flood, they moved to Wakanui and bought land in its native form, (covered in tussock) which they worked successfully. In old age they moved to Ashburton. Charlotte nursed many people through illness.[111]

Thomas was seen as having a "quiet, unassuming, sterling and thoroughly practical life" which "gained for him the highest esteem of all with whom he came in contact. They left six sons and four daughters and 24 grandchildren.[112]

Elliott

William Elliott was born in Dorking, Surrey in 1838 and became a gardener for Sir Benjamin Brodie. He travelled to Lyttelton in 1863, on the *Lancashire Witch*. On arrival he was gardener to the Hon. Leslie Lee in Rangiora. He then worked as an independent gardener for many years. In 1872, he took up a property in the district of Bennetts, increasing his land over the years. He was a member of the Carleton School Committee for two terms. He married on 10 March 1863 to the daughter of Mr. John Lewis, of Flowton, Suffolk and they had six daughters.[113]

Mr and Mrs W. Elliott

Evans

Benjamin Evans was born in Montgomery, North Wales in 1843 and was brought up on his father's farm. He travelled to Timaru in 1863 on the *Lancashire Witch*. He worked for seven years on Mr. Luxmore's farm and then bought 50 acres at Pareora. He sold it five years later and bought 500 acres, which was called Alpine Farm. He visited England in 1885. He married in New Zealand and they had nine children[114]

Mr B. Evans

Finnell

Anne Finnell was originally from England. She came to New Zealand as a governess for a pioneer family and stayed for three years before returning to England. She then travelled out to New Zealand again, this time on the *Lancashire Witch*. She first lived with the family of Hon. J. B. Acland and, while living there, met Mr John Fitzgerald who she married. They moved to Cullen Farm, Kerrytown, Timaru. She was well regarded in the district. When she died in 1916 she left her husband, two daughters and one son behind.[115] She was buried in Temuka Cemetery.

Hatton

Maria Jane Elizabeth Hatton travelled to New Zealand on the *Lancashire Witch* in 1863, a 22 year old domestic servant from Warwickshire. In her obituary it claims there were 500 single women and a matron on board. This is a big exageration! When she arrived at Lyttelton she walked over the bridle track to Christchurch. She married Mr Ockenden in 1863. They moved to the Manawatu and lived at Foxton and Palmerston North during the Maori uprisings which were very unnerving. While at Foxton they were moved to Wellington by the Government where they lived for many years. They then moved to Pakuratahi where Mr Ockenden was employed as an inspector of timber construction, while the Rimutaka railway was being built. They also lived at Masterton. After Mr Ockenden's death, Maria moved to Wellington. She died in 1935 and left a family of two sons and four daughters, nineteen grandchildren and eleven great-grandchildren.[116]

Hicks

Frances Hicks and his wife arrived in Timaru on the *Lancashire Witch*. They were well known residents of the town for many years. Frances was a market gardener and farmer. They moved to Tauranga and lived there for eight years before moving to Gisborne. Mr Hicks died in 1902 and Mrs Hicks in 1908, of congestion of the lungs. They left behind a family of eight children,[117] 37 grandchildren and four great grandchildren.[118]

Hight

Henry Hight was born in Broughton, Northamptonshire, England in 1836. As a young man he worked on his father's and uncle's farms. He married Miss Mee in 1858. Miss Mee was from Burton Latimer in Northamptonshire.[119] When he was 27 he travelled with his wife to Lyttelton on the *Lancashire Witch*. His first job was head gardener for Watts Russell at Ilam and also for Henry Lance. They lived in Weedons for some years before moving, in 1874, to Brookside.[119] That year he started farming 184 acres of land at Brookside. The land was covered with flax and raupo and was extremely swampy. There were also many pine stumps. Henry turned the land into Crystal Fountain Farm, making it well drained and cultivated with a homestead, garden, orchard and plantations. He bred Shorthorn cattle very successfully, as well as Shorthorns of the milking strain, and won several prizes. He was one of the founders of St Luke's Church, Brookside. They retired to St Albans in 1899.[119] On his death in 1913, he left a widow, six daughters, four sons, 39 grand-children and six great grandchildren.[120] Mrs Hight died in 1919.[119]

Mr and Mrs H. Hight

Holland

Henry Holland arrived on the *Lancashire Witch* as a small boy in 1863. He was Mayor of Christchurch when he helped organise a reunion of passengers in 1913 with the help of Mr. G. W. Leadley of Ashburton. The reunion was held at Ashburton as there weren't as many survivors from the ship in Christchurch, as Timaru and Ashburton. Mr Holland couldn't remember very much of the voyage as he was too young at the time. He did however remember vividly the sighting of land and the excitement on board![121]

Mr H. Holland

Fleming

Henry Fleming and his wife June came out to Timaru on the *Lancashire Witch* with six children, the eldest ones being 20, 16 and 13 years of age. Henry had quite a bit of illness after arriving in New Zealand which caused him to be out of work a lot. He was earning 10 to 11 shillings per day. At that time he had "interest in a small property." He was out of work for ten weeks and his wife was not in good health. All in all they were struggling in those first few years in Timaru.[122] Henry died at some stage before his wife, with June dying at 27 Manchester Street, Christchurch aged 79 years in 1920.[123]

Jones

Edward Jones was a native of Stourbridge, Worcestershire and learnt the trade of carriage builder from his father in England. He travelled to New Zealand on the *Lancashire Witch* in 1863 and worked for various employers on arrival, for about five years. He went into business on his own and purchased a business, Sydenham Carriage Works in 1880. He made improvements on four-wheelers, vans and steel-framed roadsters.[124]

Menzies

Miss Margaret Menzies was born at sea on the *Lancashire Witch* on 2 October 1863.

She was educated mainly at the West Christchurch School where she gained a Provincial Government scholarship tenable for two years. She then served four years as a pupil-teacher.

Miss M. Menzies

She was then at Normal Training School for 12 months and got her certificate as a teacher. She was appointed junior assistant mistress at West Christchurch and was then promoted to First Assistant-Mistress in 1894.[125]

Mehrtens

George Mehrtens was born in 1842 in the province of Hanover, Germany and was brought up in the country. He came to New Zealand on the *Lancashire Witch* and took up various occupations in Ohoka until 1868. Back then the country was all covered with flax, raupo and scrub and there were no roads in the district. He bought 142 acres and turned it into an excellent farm. He married a daughter of Mr. H. Deetjen of Hanover in 1867 and they had one son and four daughters.[126]

Meyer

Hermen Meyer was born in 1843 in Hanover, Germany. He was brought up in the country and then became a carpenter. He moved to England and had a year in a sugar factory before travelling to Timaru on the ship *Lancashire Witch* in 1863. He worked as a carpenter in Timaru for a while and then at Waitmate for some years. He then bought land at Waituna which he called Rosefield, and where he bred sheep and cattle and grew grain. He was a member of the Waituna School Committee. After 40 years in New Zealand he took a trip back to Germany and America, with his wife, spending seven months away. His wife was the daughter of John Krisle of Hanover. They married in 1870 and had five sons and four daughters.[127]

Mr H. Meyer

Prestidge

Jesse Prestidge came to New Zealand with six sons and one daughter. He moved to Hororata in 1868 where he worked as a builder for thirty-six years. He also had a brewery business for 18 years. He died in 1904 leaving a wife, eight sons and one daughter as well as thirty-six grandchildren. Three hundred people attended his funeral.[128]

Robbie

Mr and Mrs J. Robbie were married in Montrose, Scotland on 12 June 1863, just before their journey to New Zealand on the *Lancashire Witch* in 1863. They first settled in Christchurch. In 1890 the family moved to Bunnythorpe which at that time had a lot of bush. In 1908 they moved to Palmerston North. They had many children and celebrated a Golden Wedding in 1913. "The wedding breakfast over, the remainder of the day was spent in music, games, and dancing, in all of which the old folks showed that they still retain the gaiety and vigour of youth."[129]

Shipley

Burton Shipley was born at Foston, Yorkshire, England in 1837, the son of a farmer. He sailed to Lyttelton with his family in 1863 and after landing became a shepherd on a farm near Rakaia Gorge. He worked for about six years on different farms at Templeton and then bought a property at West Melton where he farmed for five years. He was involved with sheep shearing for two years and drove threshing machines. In 1875 he went to

Courtenay as manager of an estate for Colonel Brett, and stayed there for four years. In 1879 he resigned and bought land at Charing Cross, where he was one of the earliest settlers. His farm of over 900 acres was called Pine Farm. He mainly grazed sheep and grew grain. Burton married twice. His first wife died in 1868 leaving one son and in 1874 he married Miss Thompson of Northern Ireland. They had three sons and seven daughters.[130] One of Burton's descendants was also called Burton Shipley. His wife, Dame Jenny Shipley, was the first female Prime Minister of New Zealand from December 1997 to December 1999.[131]

Sinclair

John Sinclair was born in Caithness-shire, Scotland where he learned building and carpentry from his father. He travelled to New Zealand on the *Lancashire Witch* in 1863 and worked in his trade for two years in Christchurch. He had a three month building job in Cheviot for Hon. W. Robinson, which turned into 28 years! All the buildings which stood at Cheviot when the Government bought the property had been built or supervised by John Sinclair. John also worked as a mechanical engineer. Along with Mr. McQueen, he managed Lady Charles Campbell's Cheviot Homestead and Happy Valley Estates. In 1893, the Government appointed him as harbourmaster at Port Robinson. John was also an excellent amateur photographer and had many wonderful photos of Cheviot and Port Robinson. He was also involved in many clubs and committees. He married Miss Ross of Caithness-shire in 1870 and they had two sons and one daughter.[132]

Mr J. Sinclair

Wallace

Alfred Wallace was born in Treeve, Cornwall, England in 1839. He trained as a wheelwright and worked in Penzance and then London. He helped erect the London Exhibition of 1862. He came to New Zealand on the *Lancashire Witch* because of bad health. His first job was building Messrs Miles and Co.'s large offices in Hereford Street, Christchurch. In 1864 he did a large fencing contract in West Melton, with his brother. He was then employed by Hon. Colonel Brett as a ploughman and then employed by Captain Halkett. He tried farming for four years but gave up due to

Mr and Mrs A. Wallace

the bad seasons. He entered the building trade and built the school and some other large buildings at Yaldhurst. He moved to Sheffield in 1876 and worked as a wheelwright for six years. He married Mrs Mary Wollelett of Sheffield who came to New Zealand in 1874 on the ship *Lady Jocelyn*.[133]

Waring

After his arrival in New Zealand, James Waring was the manager of the Flying Cloud mine. He had a business in Auckland and then moved to Redhill for a quiet life. He died at his son's house in Aratapu in 1903.[134]

Winter

John Winter was born in Salthy, Leicestershire, England in 1836 and worked as a farm servant for 13 years, before travelling on the *Lancashire Witch* to Lyttelton in 1863. He worked for two years near Styx and then settled at Swannanoa in 1865, where he bought 70 acres of land. He increased his farm to 700 acres of land. He was chairman of the Mandeville Plains School committee for ten years. He married in 1865 to a daughter of Mr W. Stokes of Styx, who was a passenger by the ship *Randolph*. They had four sons and three surviving daughters.[135]

Voyage to Auckland

(13 February 1865 – 2 June 1865)

Voyage to Auckland, 1865

The *Lancashire Witch* made a third journey to New Zealand in 1865, this time to Auckland, under the command of Captain George King.

The ship left Start Point, England, on 13 February 1865. It had the largest number of immigrants ever brought to Auckland on one ship. Approximately 490 passengers were on board, all sent out by emigration agent Captain W. E. Daldy, Esq. The ship had received a £22,000 refit which was possibly the reason the tonnage of the ship had increased.[136] It was now a "large double-topsail ship of 1600 tons."[137]

On the voyage they passed the Cape de Verde Islands. The Equator was crossed on 6 March, 22 days out, in the Longitude 28.30 W. There were 44 days between the Equator and the Greenwich meridian which was reached on 24 April. This was a long time indeed, caused by not meeting the Southern Trade winds. After reaching 20 degrees they met with a series of S.E. gales which slowed them right down. They "ran their easting" between 45 degrees and 46 degrees south, which was quite low in the Southern Ocean. They saw Tasmania on 21 May and then the North Cape a few days later, sighting land 100 days after departing England.[136] The journey took 109 days port to port,[137] which was a very long and trying voyage for such a large and fast ship.[136] The voyage was described as "pleasant but tedious."[138]

Even though the voyage was long with a huge number of passengers, the ship was very clean and the passengers were comfortable[136] and in excellent health, to the credit of the Captain and Surgeon.[138]

During the voyage a volunteer brigade was organised to keep the passengers occupied on the voyage. They were regularly drilled by Sergeant-Major Roberts who was on board.

Also on board was Dr. Wills, the father of the famous Australian explorer, (William John Wills who was on the ill-fated Burke and Wills expedition, dying in 1861.)[139] Dr. Wills was surgeon of the ship. He received a glowing testimonial from his grateful passengers. Twelve children died during the voyage and five were born. This was a fairly low number of deaths given the number of people on board.[136] Most of these deaths were of infants.[137] The *Witch* anchored off North Head on 2 June 1865.

They had an average passage of 109 days from England. The quick voyage to Auckland back in 1856 was mentioned in the newspapers. It took only 105 days with stops at Hobart, Sydney and Wellington to discharge cargo.[137]

Testimonials

Captain King was highly respected as this statement in the newspapers shows:

"Captain King, who, as we may mention, is spoken of by the passengers in the most praiseworthy terms. Captain King appears to have gained the confidence and esteem of nearly everyone on board, for the kindness bestowed on them, during the many days they have been under his care."

There was also an excellent testimonial for Dr W. Wills, the Surgeon on board.[140]

> We have much pleasure in giving insertion to the following address, presented by the passengers to the doctor:—
>
> "June 1, 1865.
> "To W. Wills, Esq., M.D., Surgeon Superintendent, Lancashire Witch.
>
> "Sir,—We, the undersigned passengers on board the Lancashire Witch, desire to convey to you, our high esteem and appreciation of the valuable services you have rendered during our long voyage from England, now rapidly drawing to a termination.
>
> "Your courteous and cordial intercourse has entitled you to our respect and esteem, whilst to your skilful and assiduous attention in times of sickness, we are mainly indebted for our general health and safety at this protracted stage of the voyage.
>
> "Need we add, that you have secured the gratitude and admiration of all, when recovery of health has attended the result of your labours, when, at the same time, your un form diligent endeavours and solicitous care have in no small degree solaced the grief of afflicted parents, where under the Providence of God, human efforts have proved unavailing.
>
> "As fathers of families, we further desire to testify our obligations to you, for having exercised so vigilant a guardianship over our young daughters, and provided for their necessary control and supervision by a measure calculated at once to raise the moral tone of the passengers and relieve our extreme parental anxiety.
>
> "Thus, in separating, we desire that our best wishes may accompany you on your return to your home and family, that you may be long spared to continue in a sphere of extended usefulness, to enjoy a high professional and social reputation, the prestige of a virtuous life, and the consolation of declining years."
>
> [Here follow the signatures.]
>
> —*Herald*, June 3.

Bad Behaviour

There were a series of events documented in the newspapers after the *Lancashire Witch* arrived in port, as follows:

Disobedience of Orders

The following sailors were charged at various times for disobedience of orders. It appears that Captain King was very strict on his crew and suffered no fools. He had to constantly charge them through the courts for their bad behaviour. He seemed to charge his crew if they put one toe out of line.

Sailors, William Rook(e) and Alex. Matthew, were charged for disobedience of orders while in port.[141] Also Robert Walner (Warner), another seaman was charged with the same offence.[142] William Graham Clarke, the steward onboard was also disobedient, mainly because he was "not qualified to fill the situation of steward." Basically, he was incompetent. The Bench stated that Clarke should have been assessed as to his competency before the ship left London and the Captain should have seen to this, and therefore dismissed the case.[143]

Desertion

There were three sailors who deserted by the names of William Rook(e), Alexander Matheson and Robert Warner. They were "absent from the vessel without leave." They all pleaded not guilty but were sentenced to one month's imprisonment each, with hard labour. King had let Rook have ten minutes on shore but did not give leave to the other two men. King waited for them for 45 minutes. King found Rook and Matthews in the Waitemata Hotel and asked them if they would go on board the ship. They replied, "No." And that they did not care if they got three months. All they wanted was one glass of grog. It was a hard life for sailors in those days!![144]

Three more sailors Andrew Nelson, William Jacobs and James Smiles were also charged with deserting the *Lancashire Witch*. They were imprisoned for six weeks, with hard labour.[145]

George Helmers (or Helman) and Henry George[146] Page were charged with desertion. Helmers denied deserting but Page pleaded guilty.[147] He had been away from the ship for 10 to 15 days.[148] Captain King proved the desertion and Page was imprisoned for four weeks, and Helmers for twelve weeks. Helmers probably got an extended sentence for lying to the court.[147]

Henry Page was found at the house of Mary Ann Poulton, who was matron on board the ship. Mary was residing in Nelson Street, Auckland. A Water Policeman named John Jervis banged on her door on 17 June and asked her if she had seen any seamen. Constable Harnett was at the back door. She said she had not seen any. Jervis heard men talking in the kitchen and asked to go through. Mary Ann said she had no men in the house. After going to the kitchen they found Henry Page talking to some other people.

Mary Ann had made a complaint against Charles King (second officer) while acting as matron on the ship, regarding his conduct towards the single girls.[148] He was "interfering" with them! Charles King had said he would get his revenge on her once they arrived. During his statement he said he was not getting his revenge by testifying against her, it was in his master's interest.[149] The seamen had been going to Mary Ann's house almost nightly so King thought Page might be there. King had been to her door but she would not let him in.[148]

Oliver P. Sweeting was in the kitchen when Mary Ann was at the door talking to the police. He claimed Page had only come in 15 minutes before and that Mary Ann had no idea he was there. Page had never been there before, according to a Mr Terry who was also in the kitchen. Mary Ann was let off, as there was insufficient evidence against her. She narrowly avoided a large £20 fine.[148]

"Jack Ashore – at the sailors' boarding house"
from Harpers Monthly Magazine, July 1873

A Humorous Dunking!

On 4 June 1865 the *New Zealand Herald* reported that 12 passengers from the *Lancashire Witch* fell from the accommodation ladder at 4pm after it gave way. The people fell in the water. The passengers were rescued and were all fine except for getting a bit of a fright and a "thorough dunking."[150] Someone wrote into the newspaper and corrected the article.

THE 'LANCASHIRE WITCH' ACCIDENT.

To the Editor of the DAILY SOUTHERN CROSS.

SIR,—I wish to correct a slight error of your Reporter's, with respect to the accident on board the 'Lancashire Witch' on Monday last.

He states that the parties who suffered immersion were passengers, but I will now try to give you a correct version of the affair.

About 11 o'clock on the morning of the day in question, a boat-load of young Lotharios from the shore came on board to see and be seen. The ex-matron showed them every attention, and introduced them to a number of the single young lady passengers.

Elated by the success of their pre-arranged trip, they began taking many little innocent liberties, and at length were discovered on forbidden ground aft.

The "Medicus" desired them to return to the shore, but as they were somewhat slow in taking the hint, the captain was sent for, who appeared very angry, and ordered the police signal to be hoisted.

An immediate rush took place, about eighteen were on the ladder over the side, urged on by those in the rear, when suddenly—crack!—away goes the ladder, lady-killers, and all. With great and praiseworthy promptitude they were fished out, and returned to shore, amidst shouts of laughter from those whom they had attempted to captivate.—Yours, &c.

EYE-WITNESS.

Daily Southern Cross 12 June 1865

After leaving the ship, the immigrants were housed at Point Chevalier for a while before being shipped to other areas of New Zealand.[151]

An Accident and Two Tragic Deaths

A Large Fall

A sailor lad fell thirty feet down into the hold of the *Lancashire Witch* breaking one of his arms and injuring the other one. Dr Merrett attended him.[152]

Mary Cloran

A body was found in the harbour on 19 September 1865. It was identified as Mary Cloran, a passenger by the *Lancashire Witch*. Andrew Smith, a boatman, noticed her body floating in the water off Queen Street Wharf. It had been there at least a fortnight as the flesh had come off the skull. Some possessions were found on the body including two rings, one a wedding ring, and a purse containing six buttons, a small brooch and a likeness of her Majesty. Her husband Patrick Cloran, a baker living in Queen Street, had to come and identify her.

Patrick had been in New Zealand for four years and his wife had just come to join him. She was working as a housemaid. She was only 21 and had been married to Patrick for six years. They had no children. She was trying to find her husband and was very anxious and in low spirits. One of the jurors said that he had come out with Mary Cloran in the *Lancashire Witch* and remembered her complaining bitterly of the misconduct of her husband. Whether Mary had taken her own life or just accidentally fallen into the harbour and drowned could not be accertained, but it was clear there were no marks of violence on her body.[153] Another report stated that she committed suicide in consequence of her husband having had no settled home for her, and her being compelled to go out into service.[154] Whatever happened, it seems certain that her husband didn't take good enough care of her and treated her very badly.

Lothar Thiel

One of the crew members of the *Lancashire Witch*, Lothar Thiel, aged 23 years, of Breslau, jumped on a different boat after arriving in New Zealand. He was on the barque *Trieste* which went missing between Auckland and San Francisco. It left on 26 January 1866 with a cargo of breadstuff. There was concern that it had struck a coral reef in the Pacific Islands that had not been correctly mapped. A new survey of the islands in the South Seas was needed to prevent further accidents. A list of the suspected dead crew was published and Lothar was on the tragic list.[155]

Travel to Northland

The *Sea Breeze* left Auckland on 16 June 1865 for Russell with 78 passengers, 71 of whom were from the *Lancashire Witch*. They were "dispatched" to work on the Great North Road. The journey had severe weather, with gales so bad they had to batten down the hatches for nearly the whole voyage, the immigrants locked down below.[156]

The immigrants that had arrived on the *Lancashire Witch* and the *Dauntless* were working on the roads at Waimate and were to be located to their own land the week of 7 March 1866.[157]

On 14 June the town of Russell was full of immigrants and a large influx of Maori who wanted to be paid for a native reserve, and the rest arriving for a large feast. The coal mine at Russell had quite a few immigrants from the *Lancashire Witch* working on a road up to it, except they had no tools or tents yet and had to wait for the *Sea Breeze* to return. The men were described as "very steady, respectable men." Fifty of them had been sent to Waimate and Pakaraka to do roading in those places.[158]

Another 45 immigrants from the *Lancashire Witch* left Auckland on the *Ellen* for Whangaroa arriving on 11 June 1865.[159]

Mr Joseph Hare was one of the immigrants that travelled to Whangaroa after arriving on the *Lancashire Witch*. He was a boy at the time. The men were promised twelve months work at 4s per day for a ten hour day's work. The immigrants were also promised land near Whangaroa which they had to clear of bush.

The Hare family built a house of nikau but then they were told they were on the wrong section and were shifted to another place. After a year they were able to buy sixteen acres and a small house.

It was pretty tough in Whangaroa. One night a flood came down the Kaeo Valley and the Hare Family had to shelter on a rock in the night. The next morning they saw a scene of desolation. Mr Hare said, "It was a school of hard knocks."[160]

Departure of the Witch

On the 30 August 1865 the *Lancashire Witch* departed for Callao, in ballast, after staying in the harbour for some months. The owners had twice tendered for the transport of troops back to England, something that the ship was used to, but had no success.[161] While sitting in the harbour the ship *Prince Alfred* departed Auckland on 1 August and the *Lancashire Witch* was decorated with bunting.[162]

Overhaul time at about 12 storeys high. (Sea Lanes, 1935).

Stowing the Jib. The Life of the Merchant Sailor. (Scribner's Magazine, July 1893).

Voyage to Auckland 1865

Map of the Journey of the *Lancashire Witch*

(13 February 1865 – 2 June 1865)

Passengers to Auckland 1865

Passengers to Auckland, 1865

Aspden

Mr. H. Aspden and his wife arrived in Auckland in 1865 on the *Lancashire Witch*. Soon after arriving they settled in Whangaroa but returned to Auckland. They then farmed at the Mauku for about 20 years. They finally settled in Auckland. Mrs H. Aspden died in 1905.[163]

Barton

Harry Barton was born in Coventry, England and arrived as a baby on board the *Lancashire Witch* probably in 1865. He was associated with G. A. Coles and Company for 60 years. He was a member of the Waitemata Rowing Club and played bowls into old age with the Rocky Nook Bowling Club. Harry and his wife celebrated their golden wedding in 1944, at Rongotai, Wellington.[164]

Cheeseman

Henry Cheeseman arrived in Auckland on the *Lancashire Witch* in 1865 when he was 23. He was married at the time. He moved to Whangarei and lived near Kamo. His many jobs included farmer, contractor and veterinary surgeon as well as an inspector for the Whangarei County Council. He was a man of "genial nature" and was known by the name of "Happy". He loved horses and was judge at A & P Shows. He died at age 82 and was survived by six sons and four daughters.[165]

Davy

Hannah Gwilliam née Davy, came to Auckland when she was five years old with her parents. She lived in Auckland for two years before moving to Thames were she spent the rest of her life. She married John William Gwilliam in 1879.[166] She left a husband, five daughters, four sons and nineteen grandchildren when she died in 1918.[167]

Hare

Joseph Hare was born in the North of Ireland. Joseph his wife and a large family came to New Zealand on the *Lancashire Witch* in 1865 and took up land in Whangaroa.[168]

The first week there, they had to live in a hen coop as there was no accommodation. They were not a rich family, having only £5 when they arrived. Joseph was a minister and helped organise the first Wesleyan Church in the Whangaroa-Kaeo district in 1869 and was active in the prohibition movement. He was also a school teacher.[169] Joseph was on the Whangaroa County Council for 21 years and was chairman for ten of those years. He was the first person to import a marine oil engine into New Zealand. He retired to Remuera. They celebrated 65 years of marriage in 1933.[160] He died at the age of 99 years and 9 ½ months old in 1919. Joseph left a widow, eight sons, six daughters, 69 grandchildren and 69 great grandchildren.[170] He had been married three times in his life.[171] Joseph's second son Edward Hare also celebrated his 65th wedding anniversary in 1939 in Mount Eden. He asked his wife to marry him only five minutes after meeting her.[172]

Mr and Mrs Edward Hare

"We lived plainly in those days, had an abundance of food of the simplest style—we didn't even have a cow until we had been in New Zealand two years. None of us smoked or drank liquor, and in fact, we became such total abstainers that we gave up tea and coffee. Yet we were always well."[172]

Harrison

Joseph and Mary Ann Harrison travelled on the *Lancashire Witch* arriving in 1865. They lived in the far north of New Zealand. Joseph was instrumental in having the Okaihau block opened under the Homestead Act. Joseph taught in schools at Okaihau which he opened as well as other places. When Mary Ann died in 1944 aged 99 at Marangai, Okaihau, Bay of Islands, she left a son and four daughters.[173]

Jacobs

William Henry Jacobs was born in England and came to New Zealand in the *Lancashire Witch* in 1865.[174] It is likely that he was the sailor who was charged with desertion after arrival.[145] He lived for many years in the Thames area and was well known around the goldfields there. He then moved to Auckland where he worked as a boot manufacturer in Victoria Street. He moved to Northcote in about 1907. He married Mary Rattray in Thames in about 1881.[174]

Jones

Ann Jones, formerly Montague came with her first husband M. Montague to New Zealand on the *Lancashire Witch* in 1865. The voyage was very rough and according to her incorrect obituary, lasted about 6 months! This was a huge exaggeration! After landing in Auckland they travelled to the Bay of Islands, when the missionaries were there to "quell the refractory attitude of the natives." They then moved to Mackay town when gold was discovered at Ohinemuri. She was one of the first white women to "mark her footprints on the land of Ohinemuri, Mrs Mahoney being first."[175] Ann then moved to Paeroa later on. She lived in the same ancient cottage for 29 years and was very active in her garden.[175] She had five children, two girls and three boys. She died at age 82 in Paeroa in 1917.[176]

Kernot

Peter and Elizabeth Kernot arrived in Auckland in 1865 on the *Lancashire Witch*. They lived for many years in Thames where Peter was involved with mining[177] and then had a business in Auckland. Peter died in 1905 and Elizabeth moved to Hamilton. Elizabeth died herself in 1934 aged 85. They had many children.[178]

Nobes

Mr. G. Nobes who was on the *Lancashire Witch* was transported to Whangarei on the schooner *Kate Grant* with 40 to 50 other people. Six weeks later, the great Chief Maunsell died and 4000 Maori came to see his body. Mr Nobes was working on the roads in the area. One evening he saw the chief being buried and it was a sight he would never forget. He thought the local Maori were full of fun and was told that none of them would hurt the new immigrants. Some of the new English immigrants were scared though and returned to England.[179]

Routly

M. B. Routly was born in Cornwall, England and travelled on the *Lancashire Witch* in 1865. He learnt farming in Rama Rama under Mr John Martin who he worked for for six years. He then moved to Pukekohe to manage his father's farm which he eventually took over. It was 100 acres of virgin bush

Miss Routly   *Mr M. B. Routly*

when he took it up with not enough space to even grow a dozen cabbages. He cleared it so there was 25 acres of crops with the rest in grass. He had 130 sheep with lambs and twenty head of cattle. He also had a homestead with six rooms and outbuildings. Mr Routly never married and lived with his mother and sister.[180]

Saies

W. H. Saies, Senior, was born in Haverford West, Wales, in 1848, and at the age of 18 came to Auckland on the *Lancashire Witch*. He then came straight to Whangaroa. Mr. Saies, who was better known to the older Maori as Wiremu Tutu, lived his life in the Whangaroa district, where he was a friend to pakeha and Maori alike. His earlier days were spent involved in bush working, pit sawing, and timber milling in the employ of Messrs. Lane and Brown, for whom as a pitsawyer he cut the timber used for building their first two vessels. He was a general storekeeper for 44 years. In 1898 Mr. Saies was appointed postmaster and registrar of births, deaths and marriages at Saies, which post he held till a few days before his death. He was proud to be the senior Justice of the Peace in the North. He was a Freemason for 44 years, being a brother of the Zealandia Lodge and having served three times as Worshipful Master. When he died, he left one son and many Europeans and natives to mourn his loss, being like a friend and brother to them all. His funeral was large and he had "a glorious tribute... paid by his native friends, who mourned the loss of a chief," saying. "Farewell! Farewell to our great chief."[181]

Mr W. H. Saies

Sarah

Nicholas J. Sarah was born in Liskard, Cornwall, England. In early life he was a copper and silver miner. Nicholas and his family arrived on the *Lancashire Witch* in 1865. About 12 families went to the Hakaru district about 80 miles north of Auckland on arrival, including the Sarah family. They made the first roads through the bush and were then granted sections at Hakaru. Nicholas opened a store and then got an accommodation licence and sold alcohol. He was also a gum buyer who had great knowledge of the product. Nicholas died in 1894 at his residence, the Cornish Arms Hotel, Hakaru[182] and Mrs Sarah in 1918 at Hakaru. She left a family of three sons and two daughters, 13 grandchildren and five great grandchildren.[183]

John Sarah, son of Nicholas and his wife, was born in Cornwall and came to New Zealand with his parents on the *Lancashire Witch* in 1865. John was involved with a lot of sport in his lifetime and was director of Hakaru dairy factory. A lot of people attended his funeral in 1929.[184]

Taylor

Mr and Mrs Richard Henry Taylor came out in 1865. Richard was born in Birmingham, Warwickshire in 1838. He married his wife Jane Elizabeth Elwell at old Handsworth Church, Birmingham in 1859. He went to the U.S.A. in May 1863, at the time of the Civil War, where he worked as a gunsmith. He came back to England in November 1864 and two months later they were on the *Lancashire Witch* for New Zealand. It was a very stormy voyage. He was sent to Whangaroa as a military settler. He was in the flax-milling industry at Waiuku. He then moved to New Plymouth and twelve months later went to Inglewood and farmed there for 27 years. He moved to Okaiawa in 1902 and farmed there for 13 years. They celebrated their golden wedding with ten children and 30 grandchildren in 1909.[185] Richard died in 1918 and left a widow, three sons and seven daughters.[186]

Thomas

Arthur Thomas was born in Wales. He came to New Zealand in 1865 on the *Lancashire Witch*, and travelled to Whangarei. He had a butchery business and co-ran the Whangarei Hotel. He died in 1927 at the age of 81 and left behind four sons, two daughters and many grandchildren.[187]

Trenwith

John Trenwith was born in Penzance, Cornwall, England in 1826. He learnt the trade of bootmaker with his father, John Trenwith, and came to New Zealand in 1865 on the *Lancashire Witch*. He worked in Auckland as a bootmaker for five years, starting in business in 1870. He became a boot manufacturer and importer. He had a factory in Wakefield Street run by his sons, under his supervision. He became a member of the City Council in 1886 and was a member of the Auckland Harbour Board and the Charitable Aid Board. He was a member of the Primitive Methodist Church.

Mr J. Trenwith

He married in Cornwall, and John and his wife had three sons and one daughter.

Worth

Fanny Worth and her husband came to Auckland in the *Lancashire Witch* in 1865. Fanny was born in Buckinghamshire, England. After arriving they had a terrible experience. The government grant of ten acres which they were living on in Whangaroa was mistakenly given to them when it was already privately owned. They had already built a house on the block of land and then had to leave. They were destitute after this mistake and were then given a ten acre grant at Mauku where Fanny lived until ten years before her death. In her final years she lived with her daughter Mrs Adams in Pukekohe. Fanny died in 1921 aged 90 and was survived by one son and three daughters.[188]

Voyage to Lyttelton
(2 April 1867 – 29 July 1867)

Voyage to Lyttelton, 1867

Two men were preparing to travel to New Zealand in 1867. One of these men was Isaac Coates, and the other was Edgar Jones, aged sixteen years old. Isaac travelled by train to London and out of eight people in his third class carriage, three of them were travelling to board the *Lancashire Witch,* on an exciting journey to New Zealand. One of the other men was Emerson Clarkson, a native of Masham on the River Ure, Yorkshire. He was following two brothers to New Zealand, one who became a famous sheep dealer by the name of W. A. Clarkson. Emerson and Isaac became very good lifelong friends.[16]

Edgar had a very definite idea of what he wanted to do in New Zealand. He wanted to work on the sheep runs. He packed a revolver, bridle, saddle, blankets and lots of other items to take with him. He also had a list of introductions such as Sir George Grey who was Governor of New Zealand, to help him on his way.[21]

Isaac was met in London by his cousin William Coates and they went to the shipping office in London. Isaac paid 20 pounds, being the balance of his £30 second class cabin ticket. He was also told what time he needed to board the ship. He was to take a ferry steamer at the wharf, which was near London Bridge. He had all the clothes he needed in his trunk, plus a "good Yorkshire ham" which he ended up sharing between his fellow cabin passengers and the four women in second class.[16]

After travelling on the steamer with fellow passengers he was soon on board the *Witch*. A tug took the ship down to Gravesend where they stayed the night of 2 April 1867.[189] Many passengers went on shore at Gravesend. This was usually to get any extra supplies but many of the passengers came back very drunk including two women, one being Ann Swift. She was leaving her home country hoping to overcome her alcoholism but was so far not succeeding.[16]

Captain George King was at the helm of the *Lancashire Witch*. He also had his wife and family on board.[189] He was described as a fairly old gentleman who had a young wife.[189] Another description of him says he was a "blue nose" otherwise known as a Nova Scotian and that he stayed on shore after the voyage (possibly not true as a Captain King took the ship back to London) and set up a pub in Auckland.[28] The Irish first mate was a big bully and very rough. The second mate was described as an easy going and mild Englishman.[189]

The London Illustrated News stated that, "The ship *Lancashire Witch*, 1574 tons register, sailed recently from London for Canterbury, New

Zealand, with a full complement of cabin passengers and about 110 in steerage. Of the latter 85 were Government passengers."[190]

While in Gravesend the passengers saw a cigar ship which had a screw at the stern. Everyone on board wanted to see it. It had been designed by Ross Winans (an American engineer) and his son Thomas. These boats never took off as they were technically unfeasible.[191]

A cigar ship (Creative Commons Attribution Licence 3.0)

The space allocated per passenger on board the *Witch* was apparently very small, compared to later journeys were there was compulsory space size. This would have made the journey quite uncomfortable.[21]

The ship left Gravesend early in the morning and anchored off Ramsgate, Kent.[192] They weighed anchor at 4pm on 3 April. The river pilot went back on land and the sea pilot joined them. For three days they had strong gales and had to "put back."[192] Isaac describes the first night at sea when the ship had a terrible time with many sails carried away or torn and the fore yardarm coming down on the deck.[16]

On 9 April the ship started out again.[192] On 10 April they spoke with the ship *Rifleman* of Aberdeen, bound for Sydney and the next day the *Witch* was sitting off Start Point, Devon, England.[192] They never once saw land the whole journey but may have spotted the light from the Start Point lighthouse. There was still terrible weather in the Channel and head winds.[16] On 14 April they spoke the ship *William Walker*, of Boston, from London for Calcutta, 14 days out. The very next day they spoke the ship *Thames* from London for Sydney, 19 days out. The *Thames* reported experiencing very bad weather.[192] On 17 April at 11pm the wind suddenly shifted to the NE and the sea pilot left the ship.[192] It was 18 April 1867 before they cleared the channel and came alongside the Edminston lighthouse. They spent a total of 18 days in the Channel due to the bad weather.[189]

The sailors had to do their duty whilst in the channel, at all hours of the day and night. The call would be, "All hands 'bout ship," so they could tack in another direction. Whilst going through the Straights of Dover they were constantly tacking every one or two hours to avoid hitting the land which they could not see. The careful navigation meant they got out of the Channel safely.[21]

The *Witch* struck bad weather again in the Bay of Biscay.[16] On 20 April a strong gale carried way the fore staysail and this smashed one of the boats and filled the second cabin with water. On the same day they passed 60 miles to the East of the Island of Madeira.[192]

Isaac describes the sickness he had during these storms. He was so ill that he would rather be thrown overboard to end it all. The punishment of his sickness was so great. If the ship had gone back to shore for some reason he would have got off and stayed in England. One can imagine that many other passengers would have felt the same way. The second cabin was above board and would have been fairly wobbly in bad weather.[16]

The food at first was quite good but once the sickness hit everyone they could barely eat. After a fortnight of bad weather they finally came into some good weather and by this time the fresh food had run out. They had run out of potatoes and fresh meat. The beef and pork which was in barrels, and had come from America, was like eating pure salt for dinner![16]

The passengers were now generally starting to enjoy themselves since the weather had improved. On 1 May a concert was held on the main deck which would have been enjoyed by all.[192]

The 12 second class passengers had no bread as none of them could make it; even the four women couldn't make it. And it appears they never attempted to make it for themselves. A man had been employed as steward and been given a free ticket in order to serve all the second class passengers, did nothing the whole journey. He was a very incompetent steward and the second class passengers had to fend for themselves![16]

The female emigrants had the worst lot of any other group on board. There were 52 of them with a matron in charge[16] and they were all in together down the main hatch and had no portholes.[21] Their only daylight was from the open hatch and they had to climb a ladder to get onto the deck which was allowed for only a few hours each day. One can only imagine how the girls would have started to grate on each other, being in such close confines. One day it must have got too much and there was a huge noise down in the single women's quarters. The Doctor was sent for and started down the hatchway but a tin cup hit him in the face, so he came up again saying, "Let the she-devils fight it out themselves." The Irish girls had started a row with the others.[21] Isaac Coates comments that the matron "kept them effectively in subjection."[16] The Matron's name was Elizabeth Bant. Surely she had the hardest job with all the women trapped most of the time below decks and fighting with each other! [193]

Isaac wished to learn as much as possible while on board the ship and this helped him to pass the time and not get too bored. It was the first full rigged ship he had ever seen.[16]

As they approached the equator it got hotter but the condensing machine, the main supplier of water for the passengers on board, started failing. It was producing not even half what it was meant to, which was 600 litres per day. So the passengers were restricted to only a pint of water a day, which was unbearably little in the tropics. There was a large downpour in the doldrums and they caught a lot of water in a sail which was good for drinking and lasted quite a few days. If they wanted a wash however it had to be in saltwater. After arrival in New Zealand a wad of cotton waste was found jammed down the machine and Isaac wondered if someone had cruely done this, possibly in a "fit of jealousy."[16]

On 11 May they spoke the ship *Anna Sophia* from Batavia, bound for Amsterdam, 90 days out and the ship took quite a few letters with it for England.[192] One can just imagine the passengers frantically scribbling or running to their beds to get something they had already written. They were at, lat. 4 N., long. 24 W.[194]

The *Lancashire Witch* crossed the equator on the morning of 15 May at the Longitude of 25 degrees 42 minutes W.[192] Father Neptune visited and the passengers got shaved (usually this involved tar being put on the face and then shaved off with iron) and a ducking in a sail full of water. If someone didn't want to get shaved they had to pay for a bottle of grog for the sailors who all ended up drunk by the end of the day. If there had been a storm, there would not have been enough sober crew to run the ship![21]

During the journey the Doctor read the Church services on Sunday and one day when they were becalmed he read the prayer for wind. Within half an hour the wind came. At the end of the voyage the Doctor brought up the fact that his prayer had worked![16]

On 24 May the passengers and crew celebrated Queen Victoria's birthday in style, with rockets being fired and an evening concert. But on 29 May another sudden squall came up and the foresail was blown to "ribbons."[192] Edgar Jones described such a squall. Probably the one that took place on 29 May. There was not a breath of wind. Suddenly the boatswain had a look of horror come across his face as he realised something was wrong. He called out, "Let go every sail." They all rushed in a panic undoing many ropes. Even passengers helped him. They soon found out that it was a "white squall" and the wind came with huge force and "heeled the vessel over" and some of the sails were blown to ribbons. Edgar believed that the boatswain had saved all their lives that day.[21]

On 28 May, a man named J. Milieu assaulted F. Wiggins, second steward on board. The defendant was charged in Lyttelton. He acknowledged the assault but pleaded provocation which was "partly borne out by the evidence adduced." He had to pay a fine of 40s and costs.[195]

On 1 June there was very little wind but this increased to a gale in the evening which carried away the fore-topsail. For the next few days until 5 June they had terrible weather again. They crossed the Greenwich meridian on 5 June at 42 degrees 18 min south latitude.[189]

From 6 June, to the end of June they experienced storm after storm with heavy gales and head winds, making it a terrible journey for the captain and crew. This was happening when they reached the Cape of Good Hope. They again had stormy weather and then head and contrary winds for much of the time.[189] The ship constantly changed tack due to adverse winds.[16] It would have also meant that the ship was on its side most of the time, making it hard for the passengers to walk or to just relax.

Whilst in the roaring forties there was a sight that imprinted itself on the brain of Edgar Jones, aged sixteen. He saw the boatswain doing some splicing work (probably on some ropes) while the ship was lurching up and down in the rough seas. Sometimes the boat would go up at the front 40 feet in the air and then come down again, level with the waves. To add to the discomfort of the situation, it had rained the night before and then frozen, so that the rigging and deck were covered in ice. How this man could go on working without complaint amazed Edgar and stayed with him all his life.[21]

They made it through the storms and ice and on 13 July the *Witch* was off the coast of Australia.[192]

Despite the lack of water and a few other issues there was only one death on board. On 14 July, a sailmaker named Peter Jackson died from lung disease (consumption). He was older and described by Coates as a Frenchman, who used to sit and repair sails. He taught Coates how to tie a knot in the end of the twine and would tell him about his fascinating life. He used to get teased by the passengers who would sing, "We beat the French before, boys, and so we will again."[16]

On Tuesday 23 July, there was a bad thunderstorm, while the ship was off the Snares, below New Zealand. The vessel was struck forward or as

Captain King described the "report as that similar to the explosion of a canon." Another account says there was vivid lightning and the sea was striking the bulwarks of the ship and breaking them, and nearly drowning the first and second officers.[192] Edgar Jones states that although the ship had lightning rods it was struck near the anchor with a clang. Luckily the vessel was not damaged and continued on. They sighted the Snares the next day at 9am.[21] This was always an exciting time for the passengers and crew! They had made the passage in 96 days from land to land.[192] They then made it to Banks Peninsula, arriving on 27 July.[192]

The Peninsula was covered with fires as the settlers burnt the native tussock, fern and other growth in the spring. What a sight for the passengers.[21]

It then took until 29 July 1867 for the ship to arrive into Lyttelton Harbour due to head winds. The *Lancashire Witch* got into the harbour at about 8am.[192] One of the sailors had to take the ship into the harbour as they had signalled for a pilot without success. This sailor knew the harbour well and was working his passage back to New Zealand.

The passengers were all in good health on arrival, with their being only one death and two births. The conduct of the passengers was reportedly very good!

The journey took a total of 119 days and Captain King stated, "I have never encountered worse weather than we experienced in the English Channel; and our run from the meridian of Greenwich to the Port has been so protracted that, had a feeling of disgust and weariness prevailed on board, I could not have censured any one."

The *S.S. Gazelle* was chartered to take passengers from the *Witch* and their luggage to Heathcote.[192] The immigrants then came to Christchurch by the 2.30pm train on 3 August 1867.[196]

Food on board the 1867 voyage

Isaac Coates talks a great deal about the terrible food on board. He said the oatmeal and pea soup were passable but that the biscuits were so full of weevils you had to split them and shake the bugs out first before eating them.[16] The ship biscuits were hard, yellow and two inches thick according to Edgar Jones.[21] By the end of the journey they were so weevil ridden that they were inedible.[16] The flour was not much better and this was also commented on in the report at Lyttelton.[197]

Isaac didn't like the salted meat which came from America in big barrels and was like eating pure salt. The quality wasn't great either.[16] Edgar mentions that there was some tinned meat but not much variety and how he missed having vegetables. There were only a few potatoes.[21]

It appears the married couples in steerage had one live sheep per week[16] (12 in total)[21] and chickens to share between them, where the cabin passengers saw none of this. Why the cabin passengers saw none of this fresh food doesn't make sense and is not explained![16] Edgar Jones said the sheep had run out by the time they got to the tropics.[21]

Isaac lost a stone in weight after the journey and couldn't stop eating for a long time afterwards. It was as if his hunger could not be satisfied and his body was trying to gain the weight back that he lost.[16]

This sounds like an extreme case. The wife of Price on the 1863 journey became "fat and saucy," the total opposite to poor Isaac Coates.[24] The fact none of the second cabin passengers gave bread making a go didn't help their cause either! Even some male passengers on other immigrant ship journeys gave bread making and cake making a go, with great success.[72]

Many of the passengers in 1867 made resolutions to complain to the shipping company about lack of water and decent food, but they were all so glad to get away from the "wretched ship" they didn't carry this out.[16]

Old Sea Shanties

Both men who write about the 1867 journey were taken with the sea shanties sung on board. Whether there were more sung on this ship than usual, we are not sure, but they must have made a huge impression on the passengers of this voyage in particular.

The sailors would sing as they pulled the yard arms round using ropes. "Goodbye, fare ye well," and then "Hurrah my boys we're outward (or homeward) bound."

"Haul in the bowline, the bowline haul."

"We are off to the Rio Grande."[21]

There was a shanty man who led the singing during the pumping which was done twice a day during rough weather. Sometimes the passengers would help at the pump rope for up to an hour. The chant went:

> "Santiana won the day. O way,
> Santiana has gone away, so they say
> Unto the plains of Mexico."

For the order "about-ship" the mate would yell: "Let go the maintopsail halyards." An answer would come: "All gone sir." Then a yell from the helm: "Hard to lee." Then came: "Hard on the maintopsail halyards." And the answer: "Aye, aye, sir."

Then after this series of yells about 20 men would get on the rope and sing:

> "A Yankee ship came down the river,
> Blow, my bully boys, blow,
> And who do you think was captain of her?
> Blow, bully boys, blow."

Every time the word "blow" was sung they all gave a huge pull on the rope and when the rope was tight someone yelled: "Belay there."

Then all the other halyards were done! Isaac had plenty of exercise helping with all this! It happened a lot as well, due to constant head winds.[16]

Passenger Summary

Male Adults	19
Female Adults	59
Male Children	8
Female Children	2
Infant	1
Total	**89**
Farm Labourers	8
Labourers	8
Baker	1
Cook	1
Watchmaker	1
Domestic Servants	36
Cooks	5
Housekeeper	1
Dairywomen	3
Barmaid	1
Dressmakers	2
Milliner	1
Nurse	1

Where did the passengers go?

Fourteen female passengers from the *Lancashire Witch* went on to Timaru on the *Wainui* (87 tons) with Captain Bain at the helm. The other passengers were Mr and Mrs Woods and nine children, H. Jackson and wife, G. Meredith, T. Thomson, arriving 5 August 1867. [198] Many of the married couples ended up receiving wages of £60 to £65 with rations. Single men received between £40 to £52 and the single women averaged between £15 and £35. There were plenty of married couples and single men already in Canterbury and basically anymore and there would be a work shortage. The arrival of the two ships was going to satisfy the demand for single women domestic servants for about two months.[199] Another article said that the shortage of domestic servants was not going to be satisfied in a hurry and more single women were needed to travel to New Zealand.[200]

Immigration Commissioners Report on the *Lancashire Witch*

The commissioners' report stated the following:

1. The ship was in average condition in regards to cleanliness.

2. The provisions were satisfactory in quantity and quality with the exception of the flour quality which was very bad.

3. The distilling apparatus (Graveley's) had worked very badly, needing to be on 24 hours a day and still not supplying the fresh water it was meant to.

4. The single women were generally well conducted and appeared a desirable class of immigrants with the exception of four girls who were all supplied by one agent in London.

5. The arrangements of the ship were not appropriate. There were single male saloon passengers on board with a big load of single women being transported. Also in the single women's compartment, two female assisted immigrants were allowed an enclosed cabin for a payment. This was seen as not fair, as everything should have been equal for all single women on board.

6. In the compartment allotted to married immigrants were second cabin passengers, free steerage passengers, the female hospital and dispensary, and through it only was access to the store-room.

7. In the single men's compartment were the male hospital, the single immigrants, free passengers, immigrant (as in the single women's compartment) for extra payment in enclosed cabin, and besides these a portion of the crew.

8. The surgeon, matron and officers of the ship were to receive full gratuities despite any bad management of the ship.[197]

Another similar report states that on the *Lancashire Witch* and the *Blue Jacket* were "several prostitutes of the lowest grade, mixed up with some of the most respectable emigrants that we have had sent to Canterbury."

Departure of the Witch

The *Lancashire Witch* departed on 18 October 1867 for Callao in ballast at 2pm.[201] with a fine S.W. breeze.[202] Captain King arrived there in 37 days after a first-rate passage of 37 days, all well.[203]

Testimonials

Despite the passengers complaining about the food, many of them signed the following testimonial published in the Press on 30 July 1867 as they had no complaints about the Captain and head crew in general.

"A few days previous to arrival in this port Captain King received the following letters from the passengers thanking him for his uniform kindness and courtesy: -

Ship Lancashire Witch, off Ninety-mile Beach, New Zealand, July 25, 1867.

To Captain King.

Dear Sir, - We the undersigned, passengers of the ship Lancashire Witch on her outward passage from London to Canterbury, New Zealand, beg to thank you for your kindness to us during the voyage, and the manner in which you have maintained order and regularity on board without making it irksome to us.

We beg you will convey our thanks to Mr Peat and Mr Thompson for their courteous behaviour to us, and that unvaried cheerfulness which has added much to our happiness.

We are very sorry that we cannot congratulate you on a quick passage; but eighteen days spent in the English Channel was a bad start, and the incessant variable winds since we passed the Cape of Good Hope have of course prolonged the voyage beyond 110 days.

Wishing Mrs King, you and the boys a very quick and prosperous voyage home,

We remain, your very truly,

(Signed by all the cabin passengers)."

Voyage to Lyttelton 1867

Map of the Journey of the *Lancashire Witch*

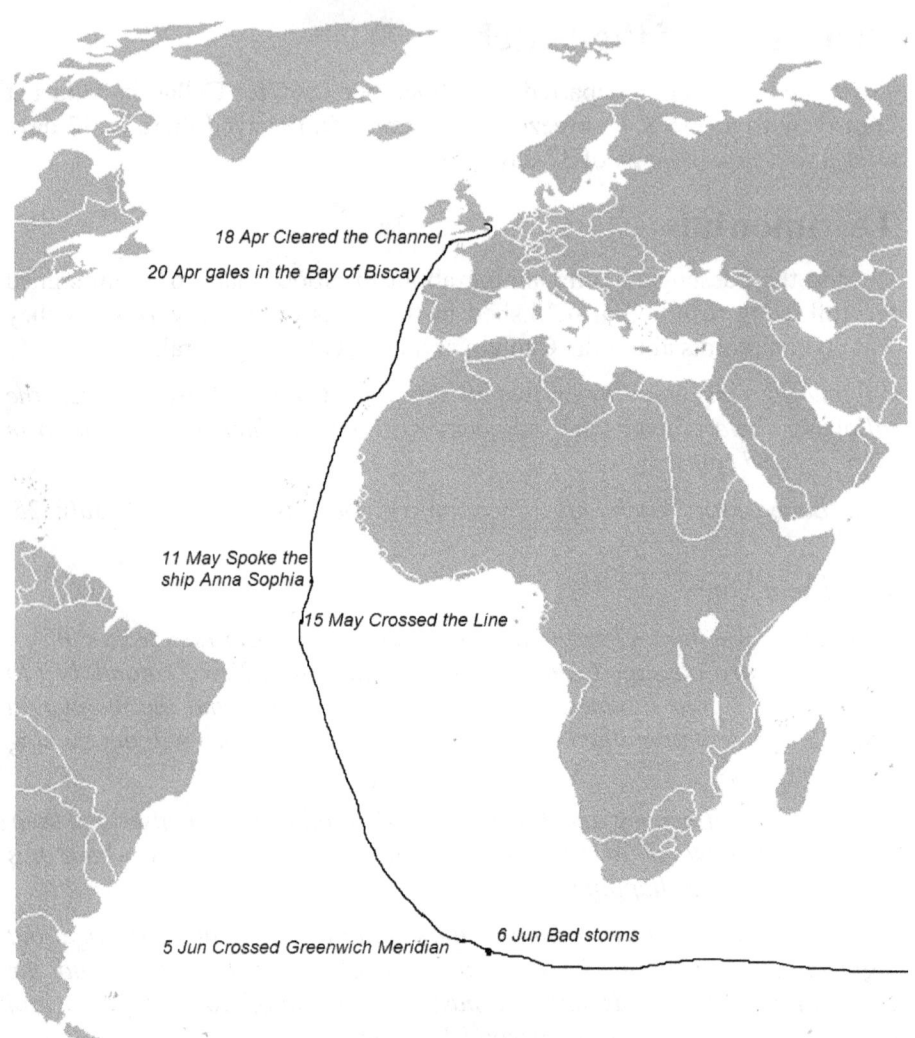

(2 April 1867 – 29 July 1867)

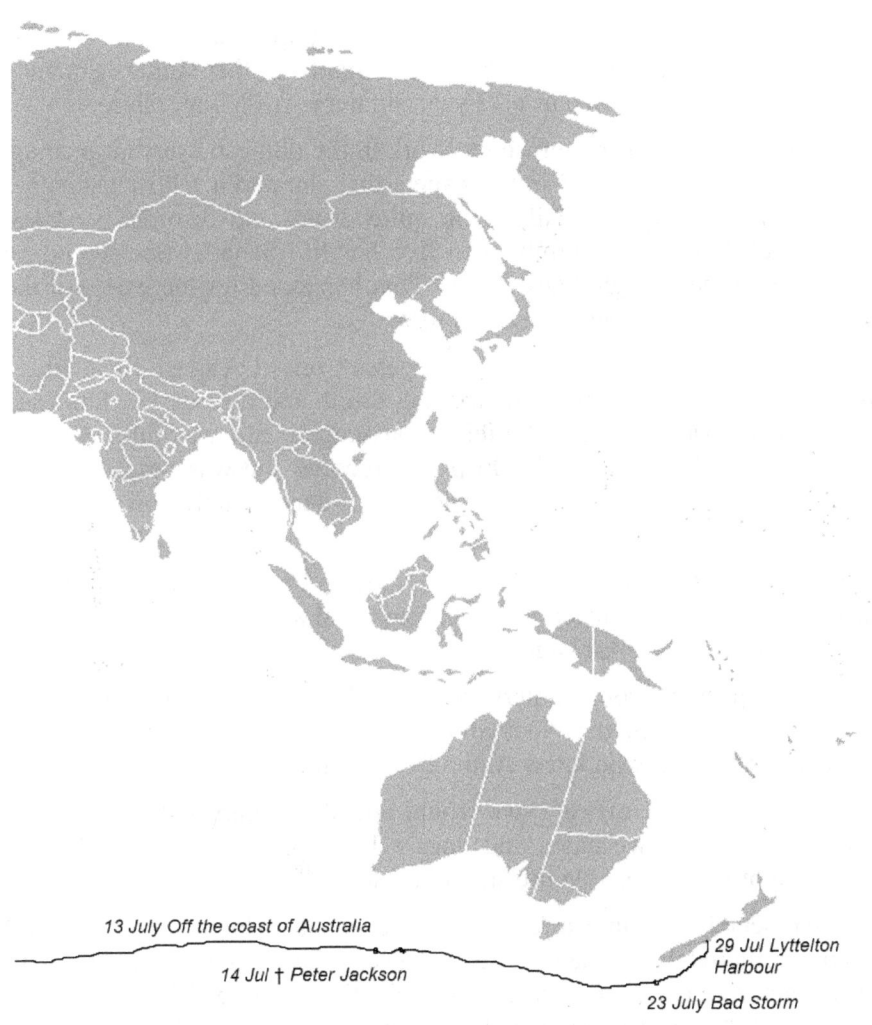

A *Lancashire Witch* - The Story of Annie Swift

Isaac Coates, passenger on the *Lancashire Witch*, was quite interested in the fate of fellow passenger Annie Swift (or Ann as he called her). So much so that he wrote a couple of paragraphs about her in his autobiography. Annie was a free immigrant in the single women's compartment and was listed as a 32 year old nurse from Lancashire.

On arrival in Lyttelton she refused to work in the domestic servant position found for her.[204] Isaac read in the papers that she and a fellow passenger passed their first night in jail, being quite drunk and disorderly. Isaac thought that Ann was determined to live her life in jail. She would be released and then brought back again. That happened for the whole of the short time that Isaac stayed in Christchurch.[16]

One example was reported in the newspapers on 12 August 1867 where Annie Swift had been charged with being drunk and disorderly. She tried to pretend she was the sister of a fellow passenger. She was fined 40s and was put in jail for 48 hours.[205] In police records she was described as 5 feet, 2 inches in height, of slight build with a dark complexion. She had black hair and brown eyes.[204]

In November 1867 Annie Swift's name appeared in a list of prostitutes in Christchurch. She was listed as having no fixed abode and was sentenced to six months in prison for vagrancy.[206]

She was "deported" from Canterbury to Auckland and a year or two later her name appeared in the Auckland papers. Isaac Coates talked to an Auckland policeman who knew Annie from Mount Eden jail.

"Oh yes," replied the officer, "we would not like to part with her. She is far the best worker we have, and does a large portion of the washing." Isaac thought what a terrible life she was leading.[16]

What happened to Annie after that? She had a baby in 1868 or 1869 possibly fathered by a man named Charles Massey whom she tried to follow back to Canterbury, but he wouldn't live with her.[204] Charles was charged with "neglecting to provide for his illegitimate child," and ordered to pay 10s per week to support the mother (Anne Swift alias Carte) and child.[207] She had another baby in 1870 and appeared with the child in court the same year. She had left her child with someone else and gone off to get drunk. The Commissioner said "he did not know that a worse character could be brought before the Bench."[208] At this time she was calling herself Carte and said her husband had left her in Auckland. An immigration officer visited her cottage and found her lying on the ground with nothing covering her. She had given birth that morning by herself.

He had to go and find a nurse and food for her and her children. She went into hospital for a while and refused to return to Auckland.

Annie Swift, a widow, then married Peter Benson, goldminer, on 2 February 1875 up in Kawakawa, Northland. On 21 May of that year she was fined for drunkenness again this time in the Thames area (a goldmining district) using the alias Benson.[209] On 18 November 1875 she was sent to jail for six months hard labour. This was her 59th appearance in Court! She only used the alias of Benson once and obviously the marriage didn't last long as she went back to the name Swift. A Peter Benson died in 1883 aged 51, probably wishing he had never met Annie Swift.

It was customary for Annie to have a "most deplorable appearance," when standing in court.[210] In 1878 she was living in a house in Chapel Street, Auckland. She went out the back and left a chair by the fire with clothes on it. The clothes caught fire but luckily the only damage was done to the chair and clothes.[211]

In 1882 she used the alias of Anne Crotchet and was still being charged for drunkenness.[212] She was charged in 1888 as being drunk with John Cooper on a railway carriage and she then seemed to take on the alias of Cooper. They had displayed "disgusting" behaviour on the train.[213]

In February 1890 a body was found on Long Beach, being that of John Cooper. Annie had the terrible task of identifying the body of her old drinking buddy and possible companion. She named herself as Mrs Ann Swift.[214]

A few years later in 1898 and 1899 she was charged with brothel-keeping. The years of rough living were starting to take their toll on her. She had a witch-like appearance now with sallow complexion, hazel eyes, grey hair and no teeth.[204]

In 1903 she was described as an old woman. She was still alive despite all the drinking and hard living. She was charged with being "idle and disorderly" and had just come out of the Costley Home for the Aged Poor and "would return there if given the chance." She was sent back into the home.[215]

No death record can be found for Annie. She may have been registered under an alias or a married name that hasn't been found yet. But all we know for sure is that she died at some stage after January 1903.

We could say that Annie, being of bad character, having no teeth, and from Lancashire, turned out to be the ultimate "*Lancashire Witch.*"

Prostitutes on the *Lancashire Witch*

There were five prostitutes listed on board the *Lancashire Witch,* sent mainly by Mr Dawson, agent in London. However, a crucial name was missed off the list, namely that of Annie Swift. Why these women were listed is never mentioned. Maybe they put one toe out of line while on board the ship and were then labelled as prostitutes or women of ill repute? Maybe they were obviously prostitutes? There was a comment that "prostitutes of the lowest grade" were on board. Whatever the case, some of them turned into respectable married women in the colony as can be seen in the following biographies.

Their names were:

> Eliza (Lizzie) Daniels
> Harriett Goddart (Harriet Goddard)
> Flora George
> Alice Small
> And Eliza Trumper, far gone in family way.

The Immigration Commissioners wrote a note at the bottom of their report on the *Lancashire Witch* which said: "Memorandum. The four girls referred to in Report were sent by an agent in London named Dawson. One at least came on board suffering from venereal complaint and all four are believed to be prostitutes."[216] Eliza Trumper was sent by a different agent. Mr Dawson owned a lodging house for servants "not of place." He had Alice Small and Flora George with him before they emigrated. Mr Marshman had references from respectable people regarding these girls and felt he was misled by people who should have been honest. One of the references was written by a Reverend. If Mr Marshman had known these girls to be prostitutes he would never have allowed them to travel on the ship.[217]

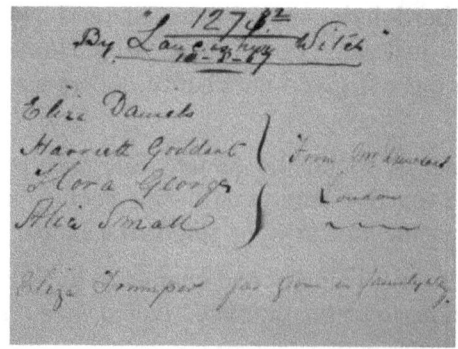

Extract of document listing prostitutes on the Lancashire Witch, 1867.[217]

The following are small histories on each woman; why they were accepted into the colony, and what their fate was in New Zealand.

Eliza Daniels

Eliza Daniels had a good reference from Rev. D. F. Wilson of Mitcham stating that she was born in London and had been in Mitcham for five years, keeping her father's home. Her father (a soldier) died on 31 July 1867 and left her destitute. She had no employer to sign a reference for her to go overseas, so the Reverend did it for her. She probably took up prostitution in desperation, as a way of supporting herself and the Rev. probably thought going overseas would help her to reform herself.[217]

Eliza didn't reform straight away though. She was named as Lizzie Daniels on a list of prostitutes who were in Christchurch in November 1867. She was of no fixed abode, as was her fellow shipmate Annie Swift.

Lizzie was "drunk and incapable" many times in her first few months in New Zealand. She was brought up in front of the bench three times in one month.[218] On her first time in front of the court she was "a respectably attired young woman" which was more than could be said of poor old Annie Swift.[219]

Lizzie was brought up on charges of disturbance and assault reported on 9 November 1867. Lizzie was asked to leave a lockup and wouldn't. She said she wanted to be locked up! She assaulted Sergeant Niall of Christchurch by pulling his hair and throwing stones at him. She had also used filthy and obscene language. She was fined £3 or to be imprisoned for a week, so in effect got her wish![220]

Lizzie's name suddenly disappeared from the newspapers and a marriage appeared in the records in 1868. Lizzie Jane Daniels married Harry Feast. It then appears that Lizzie turned her life around. No Lizzie or Eliza Feast appears in court again, only as an innocent witness to a crime in 1883 when she was living on Salisbury Street, Christchurch.[221]

Harry and Lizzie went on to have many children, possibly more than the list below.[65]

Harry George Feast	born 1875
Arthur William Feast	born 1876
Hester Feast	born 1878
Annie Feast	born 1879
Francis John Feast	born 1880 died aged 3 months
Clara Ann Feast	born 1884

Harry died in 1902 and Lizzie in 1911. They were buried in Sydenham Cemetery, Christchurch.

Harriet Goddard

Harriet Goddard had a reference stating she had worked for a woman for four years and had always "conducted herself in a satisfactory manner." She had stopped working nine months before emigrating which suggests maybe she had be involved in prostitution since leaving her job. It stated however that she had been at home during the time between leaving her job and boarding the ship.[217] Harriet kept her nose clean in her first year in New Zealand as she didn't appear in the newspapers of the time. She also never appeared on the 1867 list of prostitutes, so maybe the Commissioners and ship's officers were mistaken. There was a marriage however of a Harriet Edith Goddard to William Thomas Rayner in 1868.

Harriet went on to have the following children with her husband:[65]

Annie Helena Rayner	born 1869
Madeline Flora Rayner	born 1872
Thomas William Rayner	born 1874
Edward Bruce Rayner	born 1880
Horrace Algernon Rayner	born 1882
Herbert Welsley Rayner	born 1884
Alfred Herman Rayner	born 1887

William Thomas Rayner died on 9 October 1900 and was buried in Pleasant Point Cemetery, Canterbury. Harriett Edith Rayner died fifteen years later on 10 April 1915 aged about 65 years old and was buried in the same plot.

Flora George

Flora's reference read: "Sir, Having known Flora George and family for some considerable time, I have much pleasure in recommending her as a proper young person for your Emigration. She has secured a fair education, is honest, sober, respectable and well domesticated. I am &c. Signed M. Lewis."[217]

Flora George was another single woman who didn't seem to be a prostitute but may have had lower morals than were expected of women in those days. How she was labelled a prostitute is unknown. Maybe she flirted with the single men on board? She did, however, have no intention of marrying in her lifetime and pretended to be married for her whole life.

Her "husband" was Nicholas Smith who she lived with from 1869. They had about 9 children as follows:[65]

Nicholas Smith	born 1870
Rosa Smith	born 1871
Margaret Smith	born 1873
Mary Smith	born 1874
Alice Frances Smith	born 1876
William Percy Smith	born 1880
Annie Florence Smith	born 1882
Flora Georgina Smith	born 1884
Ada Martha Smith	born 1887

Flora had been born to an unmarried mother so she was used to this type of life and it wasn't below her morals to not marry. She died in 1930 aged 79.[222]

Alice Small

Alice Small was also known as Elizabeth Alice Small. Her reference stated that she had worked in service for a Mrs Arlington who found her honest, sober and industrious. She left due to a "little disagreement with one of the servants, and they both left together." She left the position three months earlier and was probably in a state of poverty by this time. She had been with Mr Dawson for the past three months, so whether she had time to become a lady of the night is disputable.[217]

Alice was one of the single women to go to Timaru and married William Coram in 1867 and stayed in the Timaru district until her death. There was no suggestion in the newspapers that there was anything immoral about her.

Alice and William had the following children:[65]

Elizabeth Coram	born 1869
Harriet Coram	born 1870
Jane Bruce Coram	born 1872
Sarah Coram	born 1875
William Edward Coram	born 1877

She died aged 91 years old in Timaru area in 1933.

Eliza Trumper

Eliza Trumper was "far gone in the family way" when she arrived in New Zealand from Hertfordshire, England. This was possibly after a mistake back home which she was trying to escape but she ended up being labelled a prostitute in the records! She was on board with a relation Ann Trumper aged 26. Eliza gave birth to James Trumper in 1867, with the father listed as unknown. James lived to the ripe old age of 89, dying in 1957 in

Hastings. He married Isabella Kennedy in 1896 and they had at least four children.

It appears that Eliza didn't suffer too long from her mistake. She married a respectable man in 1870 named Samuel Derbidge. They had one child the following year but it's name was not recorded. It was possibly a stillbirth.

They had many other children as follows:[65]

Catherine Lucy Derbidge	born 1872
Charles Edward Derbidge	born 1874
William Claud Derbidge	born 1876
Lilly Elizabeth Derbidge	born 1878
Herbert Samuel Derbidge	born 1880
Arthur Joseph Derbidge	born 1883
Ernest Gordon Derbidge	born 1885
Leslie Lewis Derbidge	born 1880

Samuel Derbidge died in 1908, aged 66. He was the Inspector of Works for the Lyttelton Harbour board since its formation. He had come out in the ship *Greyhound* in 1865 and went straight away to the West Coast goldfields and then to the North Island. In 1867 he came back to Lyttelton and helped erect the screw-pile jetty which was called the No. 2 jetty. He did a lot of diving in the harbour for the Provincial Government, until 1900. He married Eliza Trumper (daughter of the late Mr. S. Trumper) and according to his biography, in 1903 he had four sons and three daughters living.[223] Eliza lived to the ripe old age of 90 and died in 1939.[65]

Mr S. Derbidge, husband of Eliza Trumper

Miss Hester Hoskin – A Murderer?

Another one of the single girls on board the *Lancashire Witch*, named Hester (or Esther) Hoskin(s) had a terrible secret. Or did she? She walked into the police station and talked to Constable Alexander Wilson and made the following statement, of a crime she had committed back in England.

"I live at Mrs. Cook's. I came there on Saturday last. I had lived at Mr. Davis's, Canterbury Hotel, Lyttelton, up to Tuesday last. I had been there about five weeks. I had lived previously at Mr. Paget's, of Leithfield. I went there from the Immigration Barracks. I came out in the *Lancashire Witch*, in August last. Before I left England, I lived with Mrs. Richards, wife to a cabinet maker at Port Leven, in the parish of Breague, county of Cornwall, England. My father's name is Samuel Hosken, a miller at

Sethnes mills, at the same place. I have four brothers and three sisters. I came out by myself, as a free immigrant. William James Thomas, a travelling engineer, was murdered by me one night in March, 1867, at Port Leven aforesaid. He was my sweetheart. I had been out walking with him in the afternoon. He went home with me, and we went out again to walk in the evening, down on the cliff. I stabbed him with a large knife which I took out of Mr. Richard's bar. It was a large knife like those used by butchers. I think it was in the breast I stabbed him. I threw the knife into the sea. He fell on the cliff, and he died before I left him. I went home to Mrs. Richard. I reached there about nine o'clock p.m. I did not tell anyone. I went to bed. When we went out in the afternoon, we met several, amongst them my brother Charles. He spoke to us. We did not meet anyone when we went out at night. Next morning I got up about three o'clock, and went down to the railway station at Port Leven, and took the six o'clock train to Hale, about sixteen miles from Port Leven. Before I went to the railway station in the morning I went down to the cliff, which is about three small fields from Mrs. Richards', and saw the dead body of Thomas. I left it there. It had on a light colored small-brimmed round soft sort of hat and a black cloth coat. At the time I stabbed him, he had a grey-colored overcoat on his right arm, and when I saw the body in the morning, it was lying by his right side, partly on his body. The body was lying on the bank, rather inclining to the right side. He had on his left hand glove (light kid) and the right hand glove he had clasped in his right hand. He had on, I think, a dark vest; trousers also dark. There was blood round the body. It was just at the grey dawn when I saw it. The cliff was called the Marlow Cliff. It was a good bit away from the footpath. I arrived at my uncle's, Charles Hoskins, at Hale at about nine o'clock that morning. My uncle is a shipowner and flour merchant living at Point House, Hale. I said nothing about the murder. I stayed there until six o'clock that evening. It was Tuesday when I took the train and went to London. I went on board the *Lancashire Witch* on Wednesday, and the ship sailed from Gravesend on the 2nd April. Thomas was about 28 years of age. I shall never tell my reason for killing him. He served me very bad. We were to to be married. We had been courting about six months. A short time before I killed him we had arranged to get married, but he did not come to see me, nor did he write for a long time, and the marriage was broken off. I burnt all his letters. We renewed our acquaintance shortly before I killed him, I believe on the same day. We had no quarrel the day I murdered him. When I saw him on that day, I first contemplated the murder. I arranged to meet him purposely to murder him. I don't know whether his body was ever found, or whether I am suspected of the murder. There is no person that I know in New Zealand from the same place that I come from. The name of the clergyman at Breague is the Rev. Mr. Kidmore. He knew me well. My object in making this statement is, because I can't rest, always thinking about the murder. Since I came to New Zealand I told one person of the murder. I do not wish to mention the name of the person I told. I promised I would not do so. I don't wish to say whether or not the paper I gave to the constable was written by me. That is all I wish to say about the matter. Hester Hoskin."[224]

Hester was perfectly cool and collected when making this statement. Poison was found on her however.[224] She was remanded and the next morning several witnesses were called in to give evidence, all saying that Hester was insane. James Hebbard came from the same part of England and knew Hester's father. He came to New Zealand after Hester had already left but never heard of this murder being committed. Hester's mother was apparently in the Lunatic Asylum and he had heard one of this lady's daughters was insane but didn't know if it was Hester or a sister. Another witness Eliza Reynolds[224] said a similar thing.[225]

After searching files, Inspector Pender decided that there had never been a murder and the prisoner was remanded so that her mental state could be assessed.

While this case was going on, the Court was extremely crowded with onlookers, hoping to catch a glimpse of the "murderer." There was great excitement and one can imagine the scene.

It was noted that poor Hester Hoskin was probably going to end up in the Lunatic Asylum like her mother.[224]

Further investigation into Hester's background revealed she had been charged for setting a thatched roof on fire. The event happened on 29 April 1866, about a year before she emigrated. She was charged and held at Bodmin where she was let off on the grounds of insanity! The man named Thomas who was supposedly "murdered" had left for America about a month after Hester was charged with arson. Her friends thought they were too intimate and in her rage Hester committed the crime. She was described as "intelligent, artful and vindictive" and not really showing insanity! It was thought she just wanted to get back to England where she would have gone through a trial. She would have been thought insane and got off again.

Hester would have never been brought out if her history of arson had been known. She could have killed all on board by setting fire to the boat, and was a great danger to everyone. It was lucky she didn't misbehave on the voyage out! It was noted that there were plenty of applicants for emigration who were "indolent, incompetent and vicious persons of both sexes." Trying to filter the good from the bad must have been a terrible task for the agents in London. Often people would fabricate their lives with "forged certificates or fictitious characters" in order to get to the colonies. They would then proceed to act in the nature they were accustomed to and shame themselves again, just in a different country.[226]

Hester did finish off in the Lunatic Asylum and became a great burden on the country.[227]

Catherine Gilchrist

Catherine Gilchrist was a respectably dress female who was also a passenger on the *Lancashire Witch*. She was brought to trial for having stolen some items from the house of Mr Gilbert Butler on Manchester Street, her previous employer. These included crinoline, muslin, a hat and ribbon. She also had some stays and other articles under her bed. She was living at the house of Mr Farmer near the Lincoln crossing where she worked as a domestic servant. After being caught with the stolen goods she begged to be let off and said she wouldn't do it again. She was described as having a very respectable character. She received a light sentence of one months imprisionment due to her good character.[228]

Other Naughtiness

It wasn't just the single women who were naughty on the *Lancashire Witch* but some of the crew as well! Two of the crew used abusive language toward Captain Macaulay of the ship *Red Rover* while in port. The case was dismissed as nothing could be proved, but they were carefully watched after this event.[229]

Passengers to Lyttelton 1867

Passengers to Lyttelton, 1867

Coates

Isaac Coates was born near Richmond, Yorkshire and was brought up on a farm. He came to Lyttelton in 1867 on the *Lancashire Witch* and in 1868 moved to Auckland. He bought land near Hamilton and became one of the first councillors in the area. He was Mayor for five years, ending in 1892. He also sat on the Waikato County Council, Hospital Board and was chairman of the Kirikiri Road Board for three years. He had a go at goldmining at Thames and also had a trip back home at one stage. He was involved in large drainage and railway construction contracts and owned several flax mills. He was one of the first people to introduce mowing machines, reaper and binder and threshing machines and chaff cutting plants in Waikato. He married the daughter of Mr. P. Coleman of Kirikiriroa. She died a week before her husband. They left seven children and 26 grandchildren.[230]

Councillor I. Coates

Fowles

Charles Fowles was only a youth when he travelled to New Zealand on the *Lancashire Witch*. He was only in New Zealand a few days before he met with a fatal accident. He was riding a horse to the Avon to give it a drink and took it to a deep place where there was lots of mud. The horse struggled in the mud and Charles was thrown into the water but managed to hang on to the horse until the current took him downstream into a big waterhole. He rose to the surface a couple of times and then drowned. Quite a few people saw the accident happen but no one tried to save the boy by jumping in after him. The hole in the river was fenced off to prevent it happening again. The river was dragged that day but Charles's body could not be found.[231]

Cooper

Mr S. Cooper was born in York, England in 1850. In 1866 he sailed to Portland, U.S.A. on the *S.S. Nestona*. He stayed for a month in the state. He didn't like the prohibition conditions or cold weather so went back to

England. In 1867 he travelled to New Zealand on the *Lancashire Witch*. Cooper walked over the port hills to Christchurch and met up with his brother who was already in the colony.

He went to Hokitika after three months to try gold mining. With a restless nature he soon moved to Thames area and his first job was at Shellback Gulley for Mr Cadman at 35s per week. He joined up with the Armed Constabulary to get involved in the second Maori War, which he was involved with for 16 months. He then returned to Christchurch, where he joined his brother in the dentistry profession. He went back to England in 1870 for only six months. He got his certificate in dentistry back in New Zealand and visited Wanganui, Greymouth and Wellington before going back to Lyttelton. He then travelled to New South Wales and Queensland. He worked there as a shearer, post splitter and fencer. He had a go at goldmining on the Palmer River in Queensland and had to be armed to avoid being attacked by hostile Aborigines. In 1877, he went back to Auckland, then Hawkes Bay where he worked in a wool washing business. He then took up dentistry again. He got restless again and travelled to Melbourne and then onto Adelaide. In 1881 he moved to Invercargill. Then he moved to different parts of New Zealand, Melbourne, Bendigo and Brisbane.

He finally settled in Invercargill in 1889 where he practiced his dentistry. He tragically died in a fire at his dental rooms in 1921.[28]

Davis

Henry Frederick Davis was a native of Oxford and travelled to New Zealand on board the *Lancashire Witch*. He was a tailor in partnership with Arthur Bartholomew Clater and they ran the business, Davis and Clater on Lambton Quay, Wellington. The shops were built of wood, "having been built in the days when it was almost criminal to erect brick structures on the account of the frequency and violence of the earthquakes." They also had a shop at Willis Street which was made of the more modern brick. They had built up a good business and had well-to-do customers. Mr. Davis was described as having "trustworthiness" and an "obliging disposition."

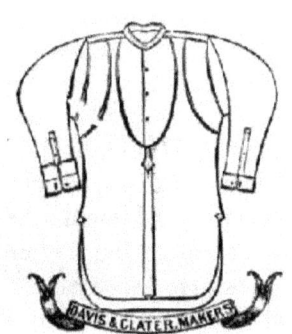

The Davis and Clater Trade Mark

He had a large involvement in public life, being an officer in the Navals and drill-instructor for the Boys' Institute.[232]

Jackson

Hinman Jackson arrived in New Zealand on the *Lancashire Witch* in 1867. He settled at Pleasant Point, South Canterbury where he lived for 18 years before moving to Hunters (near Makikihi), where he farmed for 11 years. He then moved to Timaru but didn't find it private enough, so took up farming again, this time in Summerleaze, Lower Pareora. He died of a short illness in 1899 leaving a widow and grown up family.[233]

Jones

Edgar Jones arrived in 1867 on the *Lancashire Witch* and straight away went into sheep farming. At 17 he purchased a run in the Upper Waiau and was an extremely successful farmer. He was considered one of the pioneers of the back country of Canterbury. Edgar retired in 1913. He published a book, "Autobiography of an Early Settler, in New Zealand." He was highly respected in South Canterbury and died in 1917 at the age of 83 in Timaru. He was survived by his wife and six children.[234]

Wood

Gordon Parker Wood was born in Suffolk, England in 1859 and travelled on the *Lancashire Witch* with his parents in 1867. He went to school in Timaru and worked for three years with Messrs. Russell, Ritchie and Co. and then worked for five years at the Bank of New Zealand. He became overseer of stock at the Long Beach estate and then joined Messrs. Gracie, Maclean and Co., auctioneers in Timaru, as an accountant and cashier, where he worked until 1892. He then started his own business as a general commission agent and district agent for the Massey-Harris firm and for the Phoenix Assurance Company. He was

Mr G. P. Wood

secretary to the Timaru Agricultural and Pastoral Association for many years. He was a member of many clubs and societies. He married in 1887 and Gordon and his wife had two children.[235]

Passenger Lists

The following lists have been transcribed directly from the original passenger lists of steerage passengers, with cabin passengers taken from newspaper articles. Corrections were made after research was done on the passengers.

Passengers 1856

Crew

Surname	Given Name	Age	Location	Occupation/Notes
Molison	A. S.			Captain

Chief Cabin

Surname	Given Name	Age	Location	Occupation/Notes
Blewitt	Captain			65th Regiment
28 men				65th Regiment
7 women				65th Regiment
8 children				65th Regiment
Burkett	Assistant Surgeon			74th Regiment
Peebles	Captain			11th Regiment
	Servant			Servant of Peebles
1 private sapper and miner				
Over 257 men of the 65th regiment, some of which are listed below[236]				
31 women of the 65th regiment				
29 children of the 65th regiment				
Bell	Thomas			
Bird	Felix	Private	Somersetshire	
Brown	Charles	Private	Dorsetshire	
Brown	John	Private	Down	
Brown	William	Private	Down	
Burke	Joseph	Private	Meath	
Burns	Edward	Private	Down	
Burns	John	Private	Down	
Cain	John	Private	Meath	
Carmody	John	Private		
Carr	Charles	Private		
Clareburt	John	Private	Dorsetshire	

Passenger Lists

Clear	James	Private	Queens County	
Cleary	John	Private	Somersetshire	
Cokeran	Thomas	Private		
Collard	John	Private	Wiltshire	
Conway	James	Private	Kerry	
Conway	John	Private	Kerry	
Conway	Patrick	Private	Mayo	
Cook	Joseph	Private	Somersetshire	
Cottam	John	Private	Lancashire	
Crimmins	John	Drummer	Limerick	
Crocker	Thomas	Private	Dorsetshire	
Crozier	Graham	Private	Down	
Cunningham	Patrick	Private	Limerick	
Daniels	John	Private	Tipperary	
Davison	Robert	Private	Down	
Dawson	George	Private	Lancashire	
Day	Martin	Private		
Deadman	Newton	Private	Sussex	
Dean	James	Private	Yorkshire	
Doran	John	Private	Down	
Dowling	Thomas	Private	Dublin	
Dwyer	Martin	Private	Tipperary	
Edwards	Joseph	Sergeant	Flint	
England	William C.	Corporal	Lancashire	
Farmer	John	Private	Somersetshire	
Flynn	Thomas	Private	Cork	
Freeman	Thomas	Private	Lincolnshire	
Garvey	Thomas	Private	Longford	
Geary	George	Private	Down	
Gilligan	Peter	Private	Roscommon	
Goodman	Daniel	Private	Down	
Gordon	John	Sergeant	Belfast	
Graham	William John	Corporal	Down	
Grant	William	Private	Down	
Gray	John	Private	Down	
Green	George Henry	Private	Dorchester-shire	

Greenaway	James	Private	Armagh	
Greves	William	Drummer	Staffordshire	
Gurley	William	Private	Down	
Hagan	Patrick	Private	Yorkshire	
Hammond	William	Private	Londonderry	
Hanlin	James	Private		
Harrison	William G.	Corporal	Tyrone	
Heald	George	Private	Yorkshire	
Healy	William	Private	Lancashire	
Heanon	Charles	Private	Down	
Heffernan	William	Private	Tipperary	
Hollier	Samuel	Private	Chester	
Hollinsworth	Thomas	Private	London	
Hull	James	Private	Down	
Hunt	Richard	Private		
Huntley	James	Private	Somersetshire	
Hutchison	Daniel	Private	Kildare	
Jones	Edward	Private	Louth	
Kavanagh	Patrick	Private	Galway	
Kitchen	John	Private	Armagh	
Knight	John	Sergeant	Somersetshire	
Lawler	William	Private		
Layther	James	Private	Yorkshire	
Lockerby	Thomas	Private	Dumfries	
McAllister	William	Private	Down	
McAtee	John	Private	Down	
McCormick	Hugh	Private		
McCracken	James	Private	Down	
McDonald	Michael	Private		
McGivern	Mark	Private	Down	
McGrath	James	Private		
McKensey	James	Private		
McKeown	Patrick	Private	Down	
McKeown	William John	Private	Down	
Malley	Edward	Private		
Malley	Patrick	Private	Galway	

Passenger Lists

Mancan	John	Sergeant		
Mera	Thomas	Private		
Miller	Caled	Drummer		
Miller	William	Private		
Moffitt	Robert	Sergeant	Down	
Mullican	Richard	Private		
Nesbitt	William	Private		
O'Flaherty	Thomas	Private		
O'Neill	Thomas	Private		
O'Rourke	Patrick	Private	Down	
Osmond	Robert	Sergeant	Dorchestershire	
Osmond	William	Private	Dorsetshire	
Pellican	Thomas	Private	Kelly	
Pickup	James	Private		
Reid	James	Corporal	Dorchestershire	
Robinson	John	Private	Lancashire	
Robinson	Joseph	Private	Down	
Sanford	John	Private	Dorsetshire	
Sandles	William	Private	Sussex	
Scanlon	Michael	Private	Limerick	
Shlenker	Albert	Private	Glamorgan	
Skelton	Benjamin	Private	Surrey	
Skelton	Henry	Corporal	Surrey	
Smith	Edward	Private	Lancastershire	
Smith	James	Private		
Smith	John	Private		
Smith	Walter	Private	Lancashire	
Snelling	William	Private		
Stack	James	Private	Kerry	
Stevenson	James	Private	Down	
Thompson	Christopher	Private		
Thornton	Edward	Private		
Tier	Robert	Private	Down	
Vallily	Patrick	Private		
Walker	George	Private		
Walsh	Michael	Private	Limerick	

Passenger Lists

Whiteside	John	Private	Down	
Williams	Peter	Private	Lancashire	
Williams	Richard	Private	Somersetshire	
Wilson	James	Private	Down	
Wright	William John	Private	Down	

Other passengers by the *Lancashire Witch*

Butler	Miss			
Murphy	Mr John		Schoolmaster	
Winter	Mr			
Te Hipango	Wiremu (William)			
	2 children			
Rev R. Taylor				
Miss Taylor				

Passengers for Sydney

Major Bloss				
Captain Roe				
Lieutenant Birch				
Ensign Martin				
Seventy seven men of the 11th regiment				
Two women				
Five children				

Passengers for Hobart

Detachment of the 12th regiment – 85 non-commissioned officers and men.

Passengers 1863[237]

Crew

Surname	Given Name	Age	Location	Occupation/ Notes
West	Captain			
McLean	Dr.			Surgeon-superintendant

Chief Cabin

Surname	Given Name	Age	Location	Occupation/ Notes
Salomon	Mr.			
Salomon	Mrs.			
Salomon	Daughter			
Salomon	Daughter			
Harris	Mr.			
Harris	Mrs.			
Harris	Child			
Harris	Child			
Harris	Child			
?	Servant			*Servant for the Harris family*
Carruthers	Mrs.			
Carruthers	Miss.			
Rawlings	Mr.			
Gollin	Mr.			
Otway	Mr.			
Jones	Mr.			

Second Class Passengers

Bodger	Mr.			
Bodger	Mrs.			
Bodger	Daughter			**Born on board**
Price	Arthur			
Price	Lissy			*(Arthur's wife)*
7 others, names unknown				

Government Immigrants

Married Couples – Destination Lyttelton

Surname	Given Name	Age	Location	Occupation/ Notes
Allan	George William	27	Middlesex	Painter
	Mary Ann	30		
	James	10		
	James John	Infant		

Passenger Lists

Anderson	Andrew	26	Forfar	Ploughman
	Mary	24		
Anderson	Catherine	20	T/F to single women	
Archibald	James	29	Stirlingshire	Labourer
	Elizabeth	28		
	Margaret	7		
	Elizabeth	1		
Bellman	Charles	31	Middlesex	Bricklayer
	Harriett	29		
	Elizabeth	6		
Bennett	Edward	30	Hertfordshire	Carpenter
	Esther	27		
	Edward	11		
	George J	4		
	Elizabeth Jane	2		*Died at sea 02/10/1863 Marasmus*
	Louisa S.	6 mths		*Died at sea 07/09/1863 Pertussis*
Bennett	John	26	Shropshire	Carpenter
	Mary	26		
Blyth	James	24	Forfar	Farm Labourer
	Ann	23		
Bowmaker	John	38	Durham	Joiner
	Isabella	38		
	Isabella	9		
	Hannah	4		
	Sarah	2		
Brackenridge	Alexander	25	Lanark	Joiner
	Janet	23		
	Janet	4		*Died at sea 14/09/1863 Pertussis*
Brenner	George	30	Caithness	Farm Labourer
	Jane	26		
Brinkmann	Fritz	35	Germany	Farm Labourer
	Maria	31		
Brown	Luke	36	Leicestershire	Farm Labourer
	Sarah	40		
	Matthew	10		
	Henry	7		
	Thomas	5		*Died at sea 02/10/1863 Convulsions following scarlatina*
	Lydia	3		
Buckett	William	41	Oxfordshire	Tailor

		Mary Ann	41		
		Hannah	14	T/F to single women	
		Charles William	8		
	Cass	Francis	24	Yorkshire	Farm Labourer
		Mary A.	25		
		Mary Ann	3		
	Carey	Thomas	45	Middlesex	Shoemaker
		Emily	43		
		Emily	16	T/F to single women	Domestic Servant
		Sarah	14	T/F to single women	
		Charles	11		
		Mary	8		
		George	3		
	Carter	John	26	Kent	Farm Labourer
		Emma J.	26		
		Ann Mary	2		***Died at sea 08/09/1863 Apthous ulceration following rubeola***
		Daughter			***Born on board 16/09/1863***
	Comyns	Alfred	43	Hertfordshire	*Farm Labourer*
		Rebecca	44		***Died at sea 07/09/1863 Angina scarlatina***
		Elizabeth	14	T/F to single women	
		Sarah	13	T/F to single women	
		Alfred	11		
		Mary Ann	9		
		Jane	7		
		Jasper	5		***Died at sea 22/09/1863 Anarsarca & bronchitis following scarlatina***
	Coults	Peter	23	Perth	*Ploughman*
		Betsy	22		
	Craig	John	29	Caithness	*Farm Labourer*
		Catherine	20		
	Cronin	George	28	Surrey	*Labourer*
		Elizabeth	26		
		George	4		
		Elizabeth	2		
		William	5mths		
	Crow	William	30	Warwickshire	*Labourer*
		Julia	28		
		Mary Ann	9		
		Celia J.	6		

Passenger Lists

	Michael John	3		
	Harriett	Infant		
	Female child			**Born on board** 31/08/1863
Dalton	Thomas	26	Yorkshire	*Farm Labourer*
	Charlotte	21		
Dawson	Henry	37	Warwickshire	*Carpenter*
	Elizabeth	35		
	Henry	9		
	Louisa	7		
	Ellen	5		
	Alfred	3		*Died at sea 07/09/1863 Abscesses following scarlatina*
	Frederick	1		
Shale	Ellen	20	*T/F to single women*	*Came with Dawson*
Dixon	Thomas	32	Surrey	*Labourer*
	Clara Ann	31		
	Thomas Arthur	4		
	Gilbert	3		
Dixon	Sarah Ann	34	*T/F to single women*	
Morrison	Eliza	29	*T/F to single women*	*Came with Dixon*
Doell	James	35	Wiltshire	*Farm Labourer*
	Maria	35		
	Frank	11		
	Fanny	10		
	Ann	8		
	Elizabeth	5		
	Frederick	Infant		*Died at sea 12/09/1863 Bronchitis following rubeola*
Doherty	Susan			*(Wife of Francis Doherty who paid his passage)*
Eadie	William	27	Perth	Mason
	Janet	30		
	Mary J.	2		
	Ann H.	7mths		
Elliott	William	24	Surrey	Gardener
	Elizabeth	24		
Gamble	William	24	Yorkshire	Gardener
	Annie	26		
	Herbert	Infant		
Grice	George	25	Yorkshire	*Farm Labourer*
	Sarah	21		
	Elizabeth	2		***Died at sea***

Passenger Lists

					24/08/1863 Abscesses following rubeola
	Emma	8 mths			
Hall	Thomas	27	Shropshire	Farm Labourer	
	Eliza	32			
Henderson	John	30	Edinburgh	Labourer	
	Margaret	28			
	William	6			
	Margaret J.	4			
	Male child				**Born on board** 29/09/1863
Henderson	John	39	Perth	Farm Labourer	
	Elizabeth	36			
	James J.	18	T/F to single men		
	Janet	16	T/F to single women		
	Elizabeth	11			
	Ann	4			
Hight	Henry	27	Nottinghamshire	Farm Labourer	
	Elizabeth	26			
	Albert	4			
	Anne	2			
	Mary Jane	4 months			
Holland	Robert	38	Yorkshire	Farm Labourer	
	Ann	37			
	George	13	T/F to single men	Farm Labourer	
	Mary Jane	11			
	Frederick	9			
	Charles	6			
	Henry	3			
	Sarah Ann	Infant			
Jones	Edward	21	Worcestershire	Blacksmith	
	Louisa	23			
Lamb	John	34	Shropshire	Farm Labourer	
	Jane	30			
Leader	Patrick	26	Cork	Smith	
	Margaret	27			
Stanton	Bridget	26	T/F to single women	Came with Leader	
Menzies	Charles	23	Stirlingshire	Ploughman	
	Catherine	23			
	Margaret				**Born on board** 02/10/1863
McCutcheon	George	32	Lanark	Shoemaker	
	Sarah	28			
	Charles O.	3			
Munro	Robert	29	Caithness	Farm Labourer	

		Janet	26		
Munton		Thomas	30	Leicestershire	Farm Labourer
		Catherine	33		
		Eliza	4		
		Elizabeth	4 mths		
Muzzall		Thomas	22	Sussex	Carpenter
		Rosina	19		
Otten		John	23	Germany	Farm Labourer
		Maria	22		
Patterson		William	40	Forfar	Ploughman
		Barbara	32		
		William	9		*Died at sea 09/09/1863 Scarlatina maligna*
		James	7		
		Alexander	5		*Died at sea 22/08/1863 Dysentry*
		David	Infant		*Died at sea 08/09/1863 Scarlatina maligna*
Pierce		William R	23	Lancashire	Farm Labourer
		Ann	24		
Prestidge		Jesse	33	Northampton-shire	Carpenter
		Jane	35		
		Thomas	10		
		Walter	7		
		Henry	6		
		Jesse	4		
		Edward	2		
		Mary Jane	Infant		
Prestidge		Sarah	28	T/F to single women	
Price		Henry	29	Gloucestershire	Farm Labourer
		Emily	27		
		James	2		
		Henry	8 mths		
Robbie		James	28	Forfar	Ploughman
		Isabella	24		
Rowbotham		Joseph	29	Nottinghamshire	Farm Labourer
		Jane	30		
		Sarah Jane	7		
		Joseph John	Infant		*Died at sea - 04/10/1863 Pertussis*
Shipley		Burton	25	Yorkshire	Farm Labourer
		Ann	25		
		Susannah	6		
		William	5		

Passenger Lists

Surname	Given Name	Age	Location	Occupation/Notes
	Sarah	1		**Died at sea - 24/07/1863 Diarrhoea following rubeola**
Sneddon	David	38	Stirling	Labourer
	Maria	32		
	Maria	13		T/F to single women
	Rachel	11		
	Catherine	7		
	Ann	4		
	Mary	2		
	Female child			**Born at sea 13/08/1863**
Soanes	Henry	24	Oxfordshire	Bricklayer
	Sarah	23		
	Henry A	3		
	John	Infant		
Tracey	Edward	37	Middlesex	Shoemaker
	Lucy	35		
Welges	Frederick	33	Germany	Labourer
	Hatwig	32		
	Mary Ann	Infant		**Died at sea 16/09/1863 Rubeola**
White	George	28	Aberdeen	Farm Labourer
	Margaret	30		
	James	8		
Yardley	Eli	29	Warwickshire	Printer
	Martha E	35		
	Walter B	3		

Married Couples – Destination Timaru

Surname	Given Name	Age	Location	Occupation/Notes
Aitken	Andrew	35	Dumbarton	Ploughman
	Ellen	28		
	John	5		
	Robert	4		
	Andrew	2		
Anderson	John	24	Aberdeen	Farm Labourer
	Grace	30		
Beckingham	George W.	25	Middlesex	Farm Labourer
	Emma	25		
	George	Infant		
	Ann	19		T/F to single women	Sister of George W. Beckingham
	William	11		Brother of George W.

		Emma	6		*Sister of George W.*
Belch		John	27	Lanark	Carpenter
		Mary	24		
		Duncan	Infant		
Blanchet		Auguste	21	Alderney	Farm Labourer
		Elizabeth	20		
Brasell		George	45	Surrey	Farm Labourer
		Janet	36		
		Robert	18	*T/F to single men*	
		John	16	*T/F to single men*	
		Harriett	13	*T/F to single women*	
		Louisa	11		
		George	9		
		Emma	7		
		Elizabeth	5		
Budd		William	21	Staffordshire	Farm Labourer
		Emma	21		
		Emma	Infant		
Bush		William	32	Warwickshire	Carpenter
		Martha	30		
		William	5		**Died at sea** *20/07/1863 Rubeola with parotiditis*
Butler		George	25	Warwickshire	Labourer
		Eliza	24		
Elkers		Henry	28	Germany	Labourer
		Catherine	27		
Fleming		Henry	24	Shropshire	Blacksmith
		Jane	23		
		Mary	Infant		
Gammie		James	27	Aberdeen	Smith
		Helen	27		
Goodman		John	42	Nottinghamshire	Farm Labourer
		Ellen	27		
		Thomas	5		
		Benjamin	3		
		Mary Elizabeth	2		**Died at sea** *21/08/1863 Ulcerative diarrhoea following rubeola*
		John Henry	10 mths		**Died at sea** *19/08/1863 Apthous ulceration following rubeola*
		Female child			**Born on board** *09/08/1863*

Passenger Lists

Harrop	James	25	Kent	Carpenter
	Sarah	23		
Hick	Francis	33	Yorkshire	Farm Labourer
	Mary Jane	28		
	Mary A. W.	9		
	Frances B.	3		
	Flora D.	10 mths		
Higgs	John	41	Gloucestershire	Farm Labourer
	Alice	40		
	Hannah	13	T/F to single men	
	William	10		
	Harriett	9		
	Alice	5		
	Sarah	2		*Died at sea 28/08/1863 Pneumonia accompanying rubeola*
Hudson	Henry	25	Warwickshire	Farm Labourer
	Ellen	19		
Husband	George	43	Warwickshire	Farm Labourer
	Mary	42		
Jones	Henry	30	Surrey	Farm Labourer
	Ann	29		
Koster	Behrend	31	Germany	Farm Labourer
	Sophie	26		
	Corster	10 mths		
Manning	William	32	Gloucestershire	Farm Labourer
	Hannah	32		
	George	11		
	Emma	8		
	Ada	4		
	Amelia	18 mths		*Died at sea 13/08/1863 Diarrhoea following rubeola*
Mills	Thomas	36	Devonshire	Carpenter
	Susanna	26		
	Thomas	3		
	Henry	1		
	Male child			*Born on board 16/09/1863*
Parsons	Thomas	15	T/F to single men	*Came with T. Mills family*
Mills	John	38	Lancashire	Farm Labourer
	Jane	36		
	John	2		*Died at Sea*

					05/08/1863 Scarlatina with tonsilitis
	Ellis	Infant			
Pelvin	Richard	42	Kent	Labourer	
	Elizabeth	34			
	Henry William	5			
	Richard Charles	4			
	Rose	2			
Robertson	Duncan	24	Lanark	Carpenter	
	Ellen	24			
Smith	George	38	Yorkshire	Farm Labourer	
	Elizabeth	33			
Sutherland	Hugh	31	Renfrew	Carpenter	
	Mary	25			
	Marion	7 mths		***Died at sea 23/09/1863 Marasmus***	
Sutherland	William	23	T/F to single men		
Upton	William	26	Pembrokeshire	Carpenter	
	Jane	26			
	Martha	5			

Single Men – Destination Lyttelton

Surname	*Given Name*	*Age*	*Location*	*Occupation/ Notes*
Allison	William	22	Perth	Joiner
Baker	Jonathan	20	Chester	Farm Labourer
Bates	Thomas	19	Lincolnshire	Gardener
Bates	Harriet	16	T/F to single women	
Barnes	Anthony	19	Wiltshire	Farm Labourer
Bentley	Thomas	25	Yorkshire	Gardener
Brasell	Robert	18	Surrey	Labourer
Brasell	John	16	Surrey	Labourer
Carr	David	27	Forfar	Farm Labourer
Dalton	Henry	28	Yorkshire	Farm Labourer
Dickie	Alexander	24	Aberdeen	Farm Labourer
Dow	James	23	Perth	Joiner
Duncan	Peter	24	Forfar	Smith
Duncan	David	23	Kincardineshire	Shepherd
	Alexander	21	Kincardineshire	Shepherd
Dunkley	Thomas	34	Northampton-shire	Farm Labourer ***Died on board 05/09/1863 Scarlatina maligna***
Duthie	James	26	Forfar	Farm Labourer
Evans	Benjamin	22	Montgomery	Farm Labourer
Falconer	James	25	Caithness	Shepherd

Gerrard	James	24	Aberdeen	Farm Labourer
Giles	Richard	30	Yorkshire	Farm Labourer
Gobbart	Johann	20	Germany	Farm Labourer
Gobbart	Anna	22	T/F to single women	
Harris	Edwin Charles	16	Middlesex	Labourer
Hellewell	Thomas	40	Yorkshire	Cabinet Maker
Hellewell	Grace	28	T/F to single women	
Hellewell	Hannah	25	T/F to single women	
Hellewell	Wright	18	Yorkshire	Labourer
Hellewell	James Henry	16	Yorkshire	Cloth Worker
Hellewell	John D	5	Yorkshire	
Henderson	James J	18	Perth	Farm Labourer
Hendry	Alexander	22	Perth	Joiner
Holland	George	13	Yorkshire	
Jacques	Thomas	14	Northampton-shire	
Kirk	William	23	Wigtonshire	Miller
Marshall	John	20	Lincoln	Farm Labourer
Menzies	Adam	24	Lanark	Plasterer
Mehrtens	Heinrich		Germany	Labourer
Mierhoff	Christian	20	Germany	Labourer
Muston	John		Leicestershire	Farm Labourer
Oram	Hubert	24	Somersetshire	Painter
Parsons	Thomas	15	Devonshire	Labourer
Simons	William	20	Leicestershire	Farm Labourer
Steward	William	32	Yorkshire	Weaver
Stonyer	Joseph	21	Shropshire	Labourer
Stonyer	Martha	18	T/F to single women	
Storey	William	21	Yorkshire	Farm Labourer
Sutherland	William	23	Renfrew	Labourer
Thomson	Thomas	21	Durham	Labourer
Watson	David	27	Yorkshire	Labourer
Webb	George	22	Wiltshire	Farm Labourer
Wells	Richard Berry	22	Lanark	Ploughman
Wells	William	32	Lanark	Farm Labourer
Winter	Michael	25	Leicestershire	Farm Labourer
Winter	John	27	Leicestershire	Farm Labourer
Winter	Alfred	23	Leicestershire	Farm Labourer

Single Men – Destination Timaru

Surname	Given Name	Age	Location	Occupation/ Notes
Beattie	William	26	Lanark	Labourer
Cheesworth	John	22	Cheshire	Farm Labourer
Fenton	Robert	23	Lanark	Labourer
Horler	John William	20	Somersetshire	Painter
Husband	Henry	24	Warwickshire	Farm Labourer

Joyce	John	24	Dumbarton	Shepherd
Mason	Alexander	22	Kincard	Ploughman
Ray	Charles	18	Warwickshire	Farm Labourer

Single Women – Destination Lyttelton

Surname	Given Name	Age	Location	Occupation/ Notes
Aidkin	Margaret Elizabeth	17	Cambridgeshire	Domestic Servant
Allan	Mary Ann	19	Middlesex	Milliner
Allan	Clara	21	Middlesex	Domestic Servant
Anderson	Catherine	20	Forfar	Dairywoman
Bates	Harriet	16	Lincolnshire	Domestic Servant
Beavan	Sophia	33	Middlesex	Milliner
Beckingham	Ann	19	Middlesex	Cook
Boyd	Emma	24	Nottinghamshire	Laundress
Brasell	Harriet	13	Surrey	
Buckett	Hannah	14	Oxfordshire	
Butterwick	Margaret	22	Yorkshire	Domestic Servant
Callham	Ellen	22	Middlesex	Domestic Servant
Carey	Emily	16	Middlesex	Domestic Servant
Carey	Sarah	14	Middlesex	
Comyns	Elizabeth	14	Hertfordshire	
Comyns	Sarah	13	Hertfordshire	
Cook	Emma	20	Leicestershire	Domestic Servant
Cullen	Jane	20	Lanark	Domestic Servant
Dixon	Sarah Ann	34	Surrey	Domestic Servant
Dogherty	Ann	21	Warwickshire	Domestic Servant
Druffen	Mary			Domestic Servant
Dyer	Clara	30	Middlesex	Cook
Dyer	Cornelius	4	Middlesex	
Edwards	Margaret	26	Aberdeen	Domestic Servant
Fielding	Mary	20	Cheshire	Domestic Servant
Gobbart	Anna	22	Germany	Domestic Servant
Hatton	Maria	22	Warwickshire	Domestic Servant
Hellewell	Hannah	25	Yorkshire	Weaver
	Grace	28	Yorkshire	Weaver
Henderson	Janet	16	Perth	Domestic Servant
Higgs	Hannah	13	Gloucestershire	
Howard	Ann	26	Cheshire	Domestic Servant **Died on board** 21/09/1863 Epileptic convulsions
Husband	Eliza	18	Warwickshire	Domestic Servant
Knox	Margaret	21	Aberdeen	Domestic Servant
Lindsay	Jessie	25	Fife	Domestic Servant

McFarlane	Elizabeth	29		
McLachlan	Helen	18	Buteshire	Domestic Servant
McNicol	Mary	20	Perth	Domestic Servant
McWilliams	Ann	22	Carlow	Domestic Servant
Morrison	Eliza	29	Surrey	Domestic Servant
Munro	Betsy	24	Sutherland	Domestic Servant
Murray	Jessie	24	Sutherland	Domestic Servant
Oatley	Eliza	21	Middlesex	Dressmaker
Pain	Ophelia	33	Middlesex	Dressmaker
Pain	Eliza	23	Middlesex	Dressmaker
Payne	Jemima E	28	Herefordshire	Domestic Servant
Prestidge	Sarah	28	Northamptonshire	Domestic Servant
Ridgeway	Mary A	20	Warwickshire	Domestic Servant
Robson	Jane	26	Yorkshire	Domestic Servant
Rogers	Hannah	19	Northumberland	Domestic Servant
Shale	Ellen	20	Warwickshire	Domestic Servant
Smith	Sophia	27	Lanark	Domestic Servant
Sneddon	Maria	13	Stirlingshire	
Stanton	Bridget	26	Cork	Domestic Servant
Stonyer	Martha	18	Shropshire	Domestic Servant
Strathers	Jessie	23	Lanark	Domestic Servant
Thorold	Dorothy	22	Leicestershire	Domestic Servant
Watson	Margaret	26		Domestic Servant
Young	Elizabeth	22		

Single Women – Destination Timaru

Surname	Given Name	Age	Location	Occupation/ Notes
Lavery	Catherine	21	Lanark	Domestic Servant
Watts	Annie	20	Wiltshire	Domestic Servant

Other Passengers – not on original passenger list

Adair	Robert N.			
Allen	Mr. G. W.			Was schoolteacher and preacher on board.
Bowman	J. W.			
Draffin	Mary			
Finnell	Anne			
Hadfield	Mrs C.			
Martin	Mr. J.			
Sinclair	Mr. John			
Yates	Charles			

Passengers 1865[140]

Surname	Given Name
Crew	
King	Captain George
King	Charles (First Mate)
Clarke	William Graham (steward)
Helmers (Helman)	George (sailor)
Jacobs	William (sailor)
Matheson (Matthew)	Alexander
Nelson	Andrew (sailor)
Page	George Henry (sailor)
Rook(e)	William (sailor)
Smiles	James (sailor)
Thiel	Lothar (sailor)
Warner (Walner)	Robert (sailor)
Passengers	
Addison	William
	Elizabeth
	William
	Richard
Adey	Hannah
Alderton	Charles
Alderton	Charles
	Arthur
	Fred
Alderton	Sarah
Alderton	Sarah
	George
	Minnie
Aspden	Henry
	Alice
	Henry
Aspden	James
Atkinson	Henry
	Elizabeth
Austey	Robert
Baker [Bacon][238]	James
	Ann
	Elizabeth
	Jane

Bailey	A.
	Jessie
Baker	Elizabeth
Baker	Thomas
	Anna
	Ann
	Arthur
Baldwin	William
	Rachael
	Edith
Ballenbury	Elizabeth
Bartlain	John
	Ruth
Battensley	Lydia
	Louisa
Bayley	David
	Ann
Billell	John
Billinghurst	Nathaniel
	Louisa
	Charlotte
	Charles
Bowerman	Edward
Bray	Ellen
Bray	Thomas
	Eliza
	Charles
	Elizabeth
Bray	William
Bucking	Henry
Buckston	George
	Ann
	Ruth
	Luke
Burrows	William
	Mary
	William
	James
Buxton	John
	Hariet
	Henry
Canning	John
Cares	Robert
	Mary
	Ann

Passenger Lists

	Josiah			Kate
Carey	Ann		**Dickson**	Major
	Eliza		**Doel**	Eliza
	Joseph			Mary
	Patrick			Emma
	Mary		**Dudley**	Samuel
Carley	Catherine		**Dudley**	Thomas
	Sarah		**Dudson**	Mary Ann
Cassidy	Peter			W.
Chapel	Mary			J.
Chappell	Benjamin		**Farmer**	James
	Rebecca			Margaret
	Jemima			John
	Elizabeth			Harriet
	Alice		**Fawken**	William
Cheeseman	Henry		**Foydon**	Henry
	Maria			Elizabeth
Clark	James			Harry
Clark	Patrick			Robert
	Ann			Sarah
	James			Sarah
	Winifred		**Gee**	Mary Ann
Cloran	Mary		**Gee**	Richard
Cochrane	M.		**Geraty**	Francis
Colen	John			Alice
	Mary			Thomas
	George		**Gibbons**	William
Cox	Robert			Letty
	Jane			Amy
Cumming	John			Alfred
	Mary		**Gibling**	Thomas
Daubery	Frederick		**Giles**	John
Davey	William			Charlotte
Davis	Elizabeth		**Gilham**	Frances E.
Davis	William		**Glegg**	James
	Angeline			Grace
Dawson	Alfred		**Green**	George
Deckin	George		**Greer**	Thomas
	Emma			Harriett
Deel	Joshan			Eliza
	George		**Halladay**	Samuel
	Jacob			Jane
Devey	John			John
	Mary Eliza			Thomas
	Hannah			James

145

Passenger Lists

Hamley	William W.		**King**	Rosa
Harding	Catherine		**King**	William
	Mary			Sarah
	John			William
Hardy	Daniel		**Lea**	George
	Martha		**Lee**	George
	Rebecca		**Lee**	Sarah
Hare	Richard		**Lenton**	Charles
	Joseph		**Lenton**	Joshua
	Edward			Francis
	William		**Leslie**	Alice
Hare	Robert			Mary
	Townd		**Levy**	John
	Judith			Elizabeth
	Westley			Gertrude
Harper	Eliza			Walter Dole
	Edward		**Lucas**	William
	Ellen			Elizabeht
	James		**Man**	Thomas
Harris	Alice			Ann
	Alice		**Mappel**	Joseph
Harrison	Joseph		**Martin**	Alfred
	Mary Ann			Mary Ann
Hill	Edwin		**Martin**	Thomas W.
	Sophia		**Matthews**	James
	Laura			Harriet
	Ann			James Edward
Hill	S.		**McGregor**	Charles
	J.			Sarah
Jackson	Robert			Edith
	Mony		**Mell**	Maria
	Peter			Ann
Jinking	James			John
	Sarah		**Metcalf**	Joseph
Johnstone	Nicholas			Margaret
	Margaret		**Montague**	Michael
	John			Ann
	Margaret			Patrick
	William Saril			John
Kayes	Henry		**Moore**	William
	Ellen		**Morley**	Emma
	Grace		**Morris**	James
Kennot	Peter			Richard
	Elizabeth			Sarah
King	Anne			Albert

146

Passenger Lists

	Richard		Elizabeth
Morris	John		Mary Ann
Morris	William		Sarah
Morrow	James		George
Mouldy	Horatio	**Pratt**	George
	Martha		Sarah
Moverley	Daniel		Thomas
Moverley	John	**Prike**	Frederick
	Marian	**Ratcliffe**	Peter
	William		Sarah
	Elizabeth	**Reid**	Joseph
	Richard		Emma
Moverley	Susannah		Eliza
	Francis	**Rice**	William
	Martin		Eliza
Neanan	David		William
Nobes	Aaron		Mary
Nobes	Aaron	**Roberts**	H.
	Ann	**Roberts**	Joseph
	George		Mary
	Sarah		Mary
	Thomas	**Roberts**	William
Norris	Emma	**Rotherell**	David
Norris	George	**Routley**	Elizabeth
Norris	Thomas	**Routley**	John
	Arabela		Henry
	John		Matthew
	Jane		Moses
	Joseph		Daniel
Norton	John	**Routley**	Thomas
	Ann		Mary
	Joseph		Mary
	William		Emmanuel
	Mary	**Rowe**	William
Paine	John		Selina
	Eliza	**Saires**	Louisa
Pentiluna	Alexander	**Salesbury**	William
	Mary		Ann
Peunenulia	William		Thomas
Pinhorn	Jonathan		Mary
	Elizabeth	**Sares**	William
Potts	Jonathan	**Saunders**	Henry
	Elizabeth		Ann
Poulton	Mary Ann (matron)		Eliza
	Mary Ann	**Seed**	Henry

Passenger Lists

Sever (actually Lever)	Robert			Lucy
	Elizabeth			Harriet
	Ann		Temperly	Peter
	Elizabeth		Terry	William
Shenwith	John			Elizabeth
	James		Thomas	Arthur
	John			Charles
	Edward		Thomas	Elizabeth
	Martin		Thomas	William
	Elizabeth			Mary
Simmer	Edward			Henry
	Victoria			Rachael
Simpson	Thomas C.		Tonner	James
Slanton	James			Marian
	Martha			Catherine
	Louisa			Godfrey
Smith	George		Treenon	Thomas
	Elizabeth			Emma
Smith	Joseph		Treeson	Hannah
Stanton	George		Trenwith	James
Stephens	Edward		Treworth	Eliza
	Sarah			Eliza A.
	Frances			Eliza
Stephens	Louisa		Turnbull	H.
Sutton	Bessie			J.
Taylor	Anna		Tweedle	Thomas
	Sarah		Tweedle	William
Taylor	Edward			Ann
	Sarah		Ushan	Thomas
	Jacob			Margaret
Taylor	James			Sarah
	William		Venables	George
	Thomas			Louisa
Taylor	Mary Ann			Harriet
Taylor	Richard			George
	Jane		Wall	Margaret
	Thomas		Warring	Thomas
	William			Alice
Taylor	Samuel			Edmond
	Elizabeth			William
Taylor	Thomas			Richard
	Charlotte			Alice
	Henry		Way	George
Temperley	Samuel			Mary
				Alice

Passenger Lists

	Eva			Florence
Weston	Ann			Mary
Weston	John	**Whylie**	Thomas
	Ann	**Wilkinson**	Elizabeth
	Stephen	**Wiskin**	George
	Martha			Letitia
White	Alfred			William Chorbs
	Robert	**Wortle**	John
	William			Fanny
	George			John
White	Eliza	**Woulds**	Matthew
White	George			Ann
	Eliza			Thomas

Passengers 1867[239]

Crew

Surname	Given Name	Age	Location	Occupation/ Notes
King	George			

Chief Cabin[240]

Surname	Given Name	Age	Location	Occupation/ Notes
Collingwood	Miss			
Donaldson	Miss			
Fenn	Mr. John			
Fenn	Mrs			
Hastings	Miss			
Hastings	Miss			
Brunker	Mr. Wm.			
DeSantour	Mr. H.			
Garner	Mrs.			
Gordon	Mr. Alex. H.			
Graham	Mr. Wm.			
Mansford	Mr. R. O.			
McDonnell	Miss.			
Millett	Mr			
Millett	Mrs.			
Osborn	Mr. Wm. H.			
Peploe	Mr. Fred M.			
Philpots	Mr. J. H.			
Rigott	Mr. W. B.			
Sweetland	Mr. Frederick			
Sweetland	Mr. George			
Wood	Mr. Robert			
Wood	Mrs			
Wood	Family (9)			

Second Cabin[240]

Surname	Given Name	Age	Location	Occupation/ Notes
Cambridge	A.			
Chadwick	Thomas B.			Wrote the testimonial letter.[189] Started a chemist business in Akaroa.[16]
Coates	Isaac			From his

					biography[16]
Forbes	Walter				A draper, travelling for the good of his health.[16]
Jones	Edgar				
Low	William				
Simpson	H. Mr				Did well as a bookseller in NZ.[16]
Four women		A fine sensible woman with many grey hairs and two respectable well behaved younger ladies. And a lady married to a cabin passenger but had to come out as single.			
One other		There were 12 people in second class according to Isaac Coates.[16]			

Government Immigrants

Married Couples

Surname	Given Name	Age	Location	Occupation/ Notes
Davis	Philip	39	Oxfordshire	Cook
	Eliza	41		
	Thomas	18	T/F Single Men	Laborer
	Henry	16	T/F Single Men	Laborer
Greig	Daniel	34	Fifeshire	Farm Laborer
	Isabella	29		
Henderson	Thomas	33	Armagh	Laborer
	Elizabeth	30		
	John	8		
	Susanna	6		
	William	Infant		(note on passenger list: 18 months and ? ½ rations on voyage)
Jackson	Hinman (Hinnian)	27	Lincolnshire	Farm Laborer (Timaru)
	Ann	22		
Murray	Thomas	25	Ayrshire	Farm Laborer
	Jane	22		
	Thomas	3		
	James	2		
Sheehan	Thomas	30	Cork	Farm Laborer
	Ellen	28		
	William	6		
	John	3		
Spooner	Joseph	34	Norfolk	Farm Laborer
	Eliza	35		
	Arthur	8		
	Agnes	5		
	Walter	3		

Single Men				
Surname	*Given Name*	*Age*	*Location*	*Occupation/ Notes*
Carver	Robt. Wm.	22	Leicestershire	Grocer
Clarkson	Emerson	18	Yorkshire	Farm Laborer
Clay	William	21	Warwickshire	Baker
Cross	Will Peter	19	Yorkshire	Farm Laborer
Findlay	Robert	23	Aberdeenshire	Farm Laborer
Hodges	Frankling	10	Cornwall	
Owens	William	20	Tipperary	Dom. Servant
Quinn	Thomas	18	Sligo	Laborer
Swindell	James	25	Middlesex	Watch Maker
Walker	William	20	Londonderry	Laborer
Walls	Robert	20	Londonderry	Laborer

Single Women				
Surname	*Given Name*	*Age*	*Location*	*Occupation/ Notes*
Alexander	Jane	25	Kings	Dom. Servant *(Timaru) (note: Mr Deake)*
Baird	Margaret	38	Stirling	Cook *(Timaru) (note: Elworthy)*
Bant	Elizabeth	37	Middlesex	Matron
Beasley	Eliza J.	17	Middlesex	Dom. Servant
Bennett	Annie	20	Down	Dom. Servant
Beswetherick	Elizth	25	Cornwall	Cook *(note: gone to Mr McIntosh's, Lyttelton)*
Birmingham	Mary	21	Warwickshire	Cook (Timaru)
Boyd	Jane	27	Tyrone	Dom. Servant *(Timaru) (note: W. Elworthy)*
Brodie	Ellen	21	Limerick	Dom. Servant
Burn	Margaret	23	Wicklow	Dom. Servant *(note: Gone with her brother)*
Campbell	Jane	28	Perthshire	Dom. Servant
Campbell	Helen	25	Perthshire	Dom. Servant
Clay	Sarah H.	19	Warwickshire	Dom. Servant *(Timaru)*
Collay	Emma	14		*Travelled with the Trumper girls*
Daniels	Eliza	17	Surrey	Dom. Servant
Edwards	Sarah	21	Tipperary	Dom. Servant *(note: refused to go to Timaru after being engaged)*
Eldridge	Maria	22	Limerick	Dom. Servant
Foster	Mary Ann	20	Warwickshire	Dress Maker

Frizzell	Rachel	22	Tyrone	Dom. Servant
George	Flora	18	Middlesex	Dom. Servant
Gilchrist	Cathe	19	Donegal	Dom. Servant *(Note: refused to go to Timaru after leaving England)*
Goddard	Harriet	19	Surrey	Dom. Servant
Hickey	Sarah	25	Tipperary	Dairy Maid *(Timaru) (note: J. S. Fitch)*
Hosken	Hester	19	Cornwall	Dom. Servant
Kelso	Ann	19	Down	Dom. Servant
Lawlor	Ellen	25	Tipperary	Dom. Servant
Lawrence	Louisa	25	Warwickshire	Cook
Lewis	Elizabeth	22	Wiltshire	Milliner *(note: Elworthy)*
Lowther	Emma	19	Cambridgeshire	Dom. Servant
Lowther	Louisa	14	Cambridgeshire	Dom. Servant
Meade	Margaret	20	Kings	Dom. Servant *(Timaru)*
Mudd	Emily	25	Middlesex	Dom. Servant
Owens	Mary	28	Tipperary	Dom. Servant *(note: refused to go to Timaru after being engaged)*
Purdon	Mary A.	23	Antrim	Dairy Maid *(Note: refused to go to Timaru after leaving England)*
Quinn	Maria	20	Sligo	Dom. Servant
Russell	Harriet	31	Surrey	Dress Maker
Seckerson	Mercy	20	Worcestershire	Dom. Servant *(note: Mr Malden?)*
Small	Elizth Alice	25	Middlesex	Dom. Servant *(Timaru) (note: Mrs Woolcombe)*
Smith	Elizabeth	28	Surrey	Cook
St. John	Mary	25	Tipperary	Dom. Servant
Strain	Hephzibah	22	Worcestershire	Dairy Maid *(note: Mr Buchanan)*
Swift	Annie	32	Lancashire	Nurse
Syme	Grahame	23	Fifeshire	Dom. Servant *(note: Gone with her brother)*
Tooley	Theresa	18	Middlesex	Dom. Servant *(Timaru) (note: D. MacKenzie)*
Trumper	Ann	26	Herefordshire	Dom. Servant
Trumper	Eliza	17	Herefordshire	Dom. Servant
Walls	Mary Jane	20	Londonderry	Dom. Servant *(note: gone with her brother)*

Wederell	Emily	22	Surrey	Barmaid *(Timaru)*
Wicks	Jemima	23	Oxfordshire	Dom. Servant *(travelled with Davis family)*
Williams	Emma	21	Hampshire	Dom. Servant
Williams	Prudence	21	Kerry	Dom. Servant
Wright	Hannah M.	18	Armagh	Dom. Servant

Other passengers, not on original passenger list

Surname	*Given Name*	*Age*	*Location*	*Occupation/ Notes*
Cooper	Mr. S.			*Obituary*[28]
Fowles	Charles			*Drowned in the Avon.*[231]
King	Mrs			*Wife of Captain George King*
King	Children			*Children of Captain Geoge King.*

References

1. Government of Canada, C. H. Ship Information Database. (1996). at <http://www.pro.rcip-chin.gc.ca/bd-dl/nav-ship-eng.jsp?emu=en.vessel:/Proxapp/ws/vessel/public/vessel/Record&upp=0&m=3&w=NATIVE(%27NAME%20=%20%27%27lancashire%20witch%27%27%27)&order=native(%27NAME%27)>
2. Shipping Intelligence. Arrival of the Lancashire Witch, cargo and passenger list. 15 October 1863. *Lyttelton Times* 4 (1863).
3. Shipping Intelligence. Lancashire Witch for Guam. *Lyttelton Times* 4 (1863).
4. English Shipping. Lancashire Witch burden. 30 July 1863. *Wellington Independent* 2 (1863).
5. What is a Clipper Ship? | Marine Insight. at <http://www.marineinsight.com/marine/life-at-sea/maritime-history/what-is-a-clipper-ship-2/>
6. The Lancashire Witches 1612-2012 | The Public Domain Review. at <http://publicdomainreview.org/2012/08/22/the-lancashire-witches-1612-2012/>
7. The City. Lancashire Witch Reunion. 13 October 1913. *Ashburton Guardian* 2 (1913).
8. General Summary. London, 20th January. Lancashire Witch sunk with all on board. 13 February 1879. *Evening Post* 2 (1879).
9. News In Brief. Yrurac Bat and Lancashire Witch collision. 22 February 1879. *New Zealand Herald* 7 (1879).
10. Shipping Items. Brigantine Lancashire Witch. 25 April 1879. *Timaru Herald* 2 (1879).
11. Wikipedia contributors. Packet ship. *Wikipedia, the free encyclopedia* (2012). at <http://en.wikipedia.org/w/index.php?title=Packet_ship&oldid=481049374>
12. Taonga, N. Z. M. for C. and H. T. M. Settlement in the provinces: 1853 to 1870. at <http://www.teara.govt.nz/en/history-of-immigration/5>
13. Shaw, Savill And Albion Company | NZETC. at <http://nzetc.victoria.ac.nz/tm/scholarly/tei-Bre01Whit-t1-body-d5.html>
14. Acland, J. B. A. Shipping papers 'Clontarf, A1': ships regulations and plan. University of Canterbury. Acland. (1855).
15. Lansley, B. *The Wool Clipper Glentanner: New Zealand Immigration Ship*. (Dornie Publishing Company, 2013).
16. Coates, I. *On Record; Being the Reminiscences of Isaac Coates, 1840-1932*. (Hamilton, Paul's Book Arcade, 1962).
17. Costs and Wages in Great Britain. at <http://www.rootsweb.ancestry.com/~irlcar2/wages.htm>
18. Purdy, F. On the Earnings of Agricultural Labourers in England and Wales, 1860. *Journal of the Statistical Society of London* **24**, 328–373 (1861).
19. River Shipping. Arrival of the Lancashire Witch. 14 October 1863. *Press* 2 (1863).
20. Life at Sea: Museum Victoria. at <http://museumvictoria.com.au/discoverycentre/websites-mini/journeys-australia/1850s70s/life-at-sea/>
21. Jones, E. *Autobiography of An Early Settler in New Zealand*. (Coulls Somerville Wilkie., 1933).
22. Local News Of The Month. Death of Dr McLean. 27 September 1871. *Timaru Herald* 4 (1871).
23. Diver, M. *The Voyages of the Clontarf*. (Dornie Publishing Company, 2011).
24. Arthur Hubert Price diary. Lancashire Witch, 1863. Shipboard Diaries Collection, Folder 61 3/83, Canterbury Museum, Rolleston Avenue, Christchurch, New Zealand.
25. Lancashire Witch used for transporting troops. The Morning Chronicle (London, England), Tuesday, May 1, 1855; Issue 27564.
26. Spithead, transportation of troops. The Morning Post (London, England), Thursday, May 03, 1855; pg. 3; Issue 25377. 19th Century British Library Newspapers: Part II.
27. The Morning Chronicle (London, England), Tuesday, May 8, 1855; Issue 27570.
28. The Late Mr S. Cooper. 5 July 1921. *Otautau Standard and Wallace County Chronicle* 2 (1921).
29. Isle of Wight Observer (Ryde, England), Saturday, May 12, 1855; Issue 141. 19th Century British Library Newspapers: Part II.
30. The Standard (London, England), Tuesday, May 15, 1855; pg. [1]; Issue 9599.

31. Second Opium War. *Wikipedia, the free encyclopedia* (2013). at <http://en.wikipedia.org/w/index.php?title=Second_Opium_War&oldid=577670382>
32. Letter regarding the attack on Canton. The Morning Post (London, England), Monday, March 01, 1858; pg. 6; Issue 26261.
33. Lancashire Witch in China. Daily News (London, England), Monday, February 15, 1858; Issue 3667.
34. Coolie. *Wikipedia, the free encyclopedia* (2013). at <http://en.wikipedia.org/w/index.php?title=Coolie&oldid=576491280>
35. The Lancashire Witch as a hospital ship. The Morning Post (London, England), Monday, November 15, 1858; pg. 5; Issue 26492. 19th Century British Library Newspapers: Part II.
36. Bales of hemp on the Lancashire Witch. MERCANTILE AND MONEY ARTICLE. Friday Evening. 26 March 1859. *The Sydney Morning Herald* 8 (1859).
37. The Lancashire Witch for Bombay. The Morning Chronicle (London, England), Thursday, March 22, 1860; Issue 29078.
38. Lancashire Witch, Hospital ship in Hong Kong. The Hampshire Advertiser (Southampton, England), Saturday, August 18, 1860; pg. 8; Issue 1929. 19th Century British Library Newspapers: Part II.
39. The Hospital ships. Glasgow Herald (Glasgow, Scotland), Thursday, November 15, 1860; Issue 6504.
40. Family Notices. William J. Molison born. Second son of A. S. Molison, commander of the ship Lancashire Witch. 10 April 1858. *The Sydney Morning Herald* 7 (1858).
41. 'Government Emigration.' Illustrated London News [London, England] 1 Mar. 1862: 213. Illustrated London News. Web. 6 June 2013.
42. 1877 Iquique earthquake. *Wikipedia, the free encyclopedia* (2013). at <http://en.wikipedia.org/w/index.php?title=1877_Iquique_earthquake&oldid=555618553>
43. The Earthquake Wave At Peru. The Lancashire Witch Lost? 9 August 1877. *Grey River Argus* 2 (1877).
44. Shipping. The Lancashire Witch Departs Gravesend. The Morning Chronicle (London, England), Monday, April 7, 1856; Issue 27857.
45. Shipping. The Lancashire Witch leaves Portsmouth. The Morning Chronicle (London, England), Saturday, April 19, 1856; Issue 27868.
46. LAUNCESTON. ARRIVALS. 10 July 1856. *The Sydney Morning Herald* 4 (1856).
47. The Standard (London, England), Thursday, March 06, 1856; Issue 9848. 19th Century British Library Newspapers: Part II.
48. The Taranaki Herald. Lancashire Witch fast passage. 2 August 1856. *Taranaki Herald* 2 3 (1856).
49. The Lyttelton Times. News on the Lancashire Witch. 9 August 1856. *Lyttelton Times* 7 (1856).
50. Shipping Intelligence. Port of Auckland. Daily Southern Cross, Volume XIII, Issue 950, 5 August 1856, Page 2.
51. Shipping Intelligence. PORT OF AUCKLAND. Daily Southern Cross, Volume XIII, Issue 952, 12 August 1856, Page 2.
52. Shipping Intelligence. Port of Auckland. Lancashire Witch arrived in Hong Kong. Daily Southern Cross, Volume XIV, Issue 1009, 27 February 1857, Page 2.
53. Shipping Intelligence. Port Of Auckland. 25 June 1862. *Daily Southern Cross* 3 (1862).
54. 65th (2nd Yorkshire, North Riding) Regiment of Foot. *Wikipedia, the free encyclopedia* (2013). at <http://en.wikipedia.org/w/index.php?title=65th_(2nd_Yorkshire,_North_Riding)_Regiment_of_Foot&oldid=580361833>
55. Ormond | NZETC. John Farmer. at <http://nzetc.victoria.ac.nz//tm/scholarly/tei-Cyc02Cycl-t1-body1-d3-d6-d3.html>
56. Home Rule. Daniel Goodman. 17 May 1911. *Wanganui Chronicle* 8 (1911).
57. Personal Items. William Grant. 13 May 1911. *New Zealand Herald* 8 (1911).
58. James Grey, alias Gaffney, alias Lee. Criminal Calendar. 5 October 1878. *New Zealand Herald* 4 (1878).
59. Mr. W. G. Harrison. Hawke's Bay Herald, Volume XXI, Issue 5306, 13 February 1879, Page 2.
60. William Greer Harrison. Hawke's Bay Herald, Volume XXI, Issue 5305, 12 February 1879, Page 2.
61. Local And General News. Charles Heenan. 4 December 1905. *New Zealand Herald* 4 5 (1905).

62. Taonga, N. Z. M. for C. and H. T. M. Hipango, Hoani Wiremu. at <http://www.teara.govt.nz/en/biographies/1h24/hipango-hoani-wiremu>
63. Taonga, N. Z. M. for C. and H. T. M. Taylor, Richard. at <http://www.teara.govt.nz/en/biographies/1t22/taylor-richard>
64. Supreme Court Calendar. Edward Thornton. 1856 on Lancashire Witch. 1 January 1874. *Daily Southern Cross* 3 (1874).
65. Birth, Death and Marriage Historical Records. at <https://bdmhistoricalrecords.dia.govt.nz/Home/>
66. Extorts. Lancashire Witch to be sent out after the Accrington. 4 August 1863. *Wellington Independent* 2 (1863).
67. Shipping Intelligence. Lancashire Witch still delayed. 17 October 1863. *Lyttelton Times* 4 (1863).
68. David Carr Diary. Lancashire Witch, 1863. ARC 1993.67. Canterbury Museum, Christchurch.
69. Health Commissioners (Timaru) to Provincial Secretary - Commissioners report Lancashire Witch - 2/11/1863 (R22192886) Christchurch Office. Archives New Zealand.
70. Henry Thorne Shepherd, diary on board Lancashire Witch, 1863. MS-Papers-0501-1. Alexander Turnbull Library, Wellington, New Zealand.
71. Lancashire Witch spoken with. The Standard (London, England), Thursday, October 15, 1863; pg. 8; Issue 12224. 19th Century British Library Newspapers: Part II.
72. Craymer, Alfred William, 1862-1863 Diary of a voyage from England to New Zealand, 5 Dec 1862 - 13 Mar 1863. Alexander Turnbull Library, Reference qMS-0585.
73. Resident Magistrate's Court. Robert W. Greerson, quartermaster. 20 October 1863. *Lyttelton Times* 4 (1863).
74. To-day's Celebrations. Lancashire Witch one of the first four ships to South Canterbury. 14 January 1909. *Press* 8 (1909).
75. Heathcote River. Lancashire Witch, did not touch Otago. 29 October 1863. *Lyttelton Times* 4 (1863).
76. Summary Of Shipping News. Summary of journey to Lyttelton. 14 November 1863. *Lyttelton Times* 3 (1863).
77. Shipping Intelligence. Lancashire Witch landed 103 passengers at Timaru. 20 October 1863. *Lyttelton Times* 4 (1863).
78. Doctor Donald to Provincial Secretary - Immigration Commissioners report, Lancashire Witch - 2/11/1863 (R22192885). Christchurch Office. Archives New Zealand.
79. Quarantine Regulations. Editorial. The Lyttelton Times. Saturday, October 24, 1863. *Lyttelton Times* 4 (1863).
80. Town And Country. Lancashire Witch and Victory landed in Timaru. 20 October 1863. *Lyttelton Times* 4 (1863).
81. Town And Country. James Creed, desertion. 10 December 1863. *Lyttelton Times* 4 (1863).
82. 'John Linnell, Esq., R. A., the Landscape Painter, Has Forwarded to the National Life-boat Institution a Donation of £50.' Illustrated London News [London, England] 30 Jan. 1864: 103. Illustrated London News. Web. 6 June 2013.
83. Lancashire Witch. 7 November 1863. *Press* 3 (1863).
84. Town And Country. Illness of Dr. Donald. 22 October 1863. *Lyttelton Times* 4 (1863).
85. Brooks to Provincial Secretary - Immigrants per Lancashire Witch - 2/11/1863 (R22192887). Christchurch Office. Archives New Zealand.
86. The Newly Arrived Immigrants. The Lyttelton Times. Saturday, October 17, 1863. Town And Country. *Lyttelton Times* 4 (1863).
87. Bad Immigration arrangements for hte Lancashire Witch. Editorial. The Lyttelton Times. Tuesday, October 20, 1863. *Lyttelton Times* 4 (1863).
88. A. Back (Immigration) to Provincial Secretary - an immigrant landed from Lancashire Witch contrary to health regulations - 19/10/1863 (R22192804). Christchurch Office. Archives New Zealand.
89. Town And Country. Lunatic on the Lancashire Witch. 31 October 1863. *Lyttelton Times* 4 (1863).
90. Town and Country. Lancashire Witch possibly a wool ship. 3 November 1863. *Lyttelton Times* 4 (1863).
91. Shipmates Reunite. Passengers by Lancashire Witch. 18 October 1913. *Press* 14 (1913).

92. Farmers | NZETC. Andrew Aitken. at <http://nzetc.victoria.ac.nz//tm/scholarly/tei-Cyc03Cycl-t1-body1-d6-d107-d2.html>
93. Mr George William Allan. 28 September 1914. *Press* 10 (1914).
94. Farmers | NZETC. Andrew Anderson. at <http://nzetc.victoria.ac.nz//tm/scholarly/tei-Cyc03Cycl-t1-body1-d6-d15-d2.html>
95. Farmers | NZETC. William John Beattie. at <http://nzetc.victoria.ac.nz//tm/scholarly/tei-Cyc03Cycl-t1-body1-d6-d94-d2.html>
96. Obituary. Mr John Bennett. 12 March 1898. *Ellesmere Guardian* 2 (1898).
97. Mr. Peter A. Blyth | NZETC. at <http://nzetc.victoria.ac.nz//tm/scholarly/tei-Cyc04Cycl-t1-body1-d7-d61-d13.html>
98. Brasell, John | NZETC. at <http://nzetc.victoria.ac.nz//tm/scholarly/tei-Cyc04Cycl-t1-body1-d5-d10-d13.html>
99. Omnium Gatherum. Mrs George Beckingham. 14 December 1903. *Otago Daily Times* 8 (1903).
100. Personal Matters. George Beckingham. 24 October 1906. *Wairarapa Daily Times* 5 (1906).
101. Farmers | NZETC. William Budd. at <http://nzetc.victoria.ac.nz//tm/scholarly/tei-Cyc03Cycl-t1-body1-d6-d93-d2.html>
102. Levels County Council | NZETC. George Butler. at <http://nzetc.victoria.ac.nz//tm/scholarly/tei-Cyc03Cycl-t1-body1-d7-d1-d6.html>
103. Professional, Commercial And Industrial | NZETC. George Thomas Carey. at <http://nzetc.victoria.ac.nz//tm/scholarly/tei-Cyc03Cycl-t1-body1-d4-d1-d2.html>
104. Obituary. Mrs Cass. 10 May 1904. *Press* 8 (1904).
105. Obituary. Mr John Collins. 11 August 1922. *Auckland Star* 6 (1922).
106. Obituary. Mr. John Collins. 12 August 1922. *New Zealand Herald* 10 (1922).
107. Mrs Craig. 19 December 1911. *Press* 8 (1911).
108. Mr John Craig. 8 February 1906. *Press* 7 (1906).
109. Obituary. Mr. George Denis Cronin. 13 July 1899. *New Zealand Tablet* 19 (1899).
110. Obituary. Mrs C. Dalton. 24 July 1919. *Ashburton Guardian* 5 (1919).
111. Women's Corner. Charlotte Dalton. 24 July 1919. *Press* 2 (1919).
112. Obituary. Mr Thomas Dalton. 24 September 1913. *Press* 7 (1913).
113. Farmers | NZETC. Mr and Mrs Elliott. at <http://nzetc.victoria.ac.nz//tm/scholarly/tei-Cyc03Cycl-t1-body1-d4-d15-d2.html>
114. Farmers | NZETC, Benjamin Evans. at <http://nzetc.victoria.ac.nz//tm/scholarly/tei-Cyc03Cycl-t1-body1-d7-d13-d2.html>
115. Obituary. Mrs John Fitzgerald. 18 December 1916. *Press* 8 (1916).
116. Obituary. Mrs W. Ockenden. 16 March 1935. *Evening Post* 11 (1935).
117. Mrs Francis Hicks. 19 September 1908. *Poverty Bay Herald* 4 (1908).
118. Mr. Francis Hicks. Poverty Bay Herald. Published Every Evening. Gisborne, Monday Feb. 10, 1902. The Colony's Commerce. *Poverty Bay Herald* 2 (1902).
119. Obituary. Mrs. H. Hight. 19 May 1919. *Ashburton Guardian* 6 (1919).
120. Obituary. Henry Hight. 23 July 1913. *Ellesmere Guardian* 3 (1913).
121. Local And General. Reunion. 26 September 1913. *Ashburton Guardian* 4 (1913).
122. Government Enquiry Into The Unemployed Agitation. Henry Fleming. 23 August 1883. *Timaru Herald* 3 (1883).
123. Death. Mrs Henry Fleming. 29 May 1920. *Press* 11 (1920).
124. Professional, Commercial And Industrial | NZETC. Edward Jones. at <http://nzetc.victoria.ac.nz//tm/scholarly/tei-Cyc03Cycl-t1-body1-d3-d59-d2.html>
125. Primary Schools | NZETC. Margaret Menzies. at <http://nzetc.victoria.ac.nz/tm/scholarly/tei-Cyc03Cycl-t1-body1-d3-d20-d24.html#name-420740-mention>
126. Farmers | NZETC. George Mehrtens. at <http://nzetc.victoria.ac.nz//tm/scholarly/tei-Cyc03Cycl-t1-body1-d4-d22-d2.html>
127. Meyer, Herman | NZETC. at <http://nzetc.victoria.ac.nz//tm/scholarly/tei-Cyc03Cycl-t1-body1-d7-d22-d4.html#name-423731-mention>
128. News Of The Day. Mr Jesse Prestidge. 14 July 1904. *Press* 4 (1904).
129. Social And Personal. Mr and Mrs J. Robbie. 16 June 1913. *Dominion* 2 (1913).
130. Farmers | NZETC. Burton Shipley. at <http://nzetc.victoria.ac.nz//tm/scholarly/tei-Cyc03Cycl-t1-body1-d6-d26-d2.html#name-422527-mention>

131. Jenny Shipley. *Wikipedia, the free encyclopedia* (2013). at <http://en.wikipedia.org/w/index.php?title=Jenny_Shipley&oldid=578030835>
132. Port Robinson | NZETC. John Sinclair. at <http://nzetc.victoria.ac.nz/tm/scholarly/tei-Cyc03Cycl-t1-body1-d4-d37.html>
133. Farmers | NZETC. Alfred Wallace. at <http://nzetc.victoria.ac.nz//tm/scholarly/tei-Cyc03Cycl-t1-body1-d6-d40-d2.html>
134. Dying Cake-walk. James Waring. 30 September 1903. *Auckland Star* 1 (1903).
135. Farmers | NZETC. John Winter. at <http://nzetc.victoria.ac.nz//tm/scholarly/tei-Cyc03Cycl-t1-body1-d4-d21-d2.html>
136. Arrival of the Lancashire Witch. The Southern Cross. Saturday June 3rd 1865, page 4.
137. Fifty Years Ago. Ship Lancashire Witch. Five Hundred Passengers. 3 June 1915. *New Zealand Herald* 11 (1915).
138. Lancashire Witch arrival. 3 June 1865. *New Zealand Herald* 5 (1865).
139. William John Wills. *Wikipedia, the free encyclopedia* (2013). at <http://en.wikipedia.org/w/index.php?title=William_John_Wills&oldid=557676025>
140. Port Of Auckland. Arrival of the Lancashire Witch. 7 June 1865. *New Zealand Herald* 7 (1865).
141. Papers Past — Daily Southern Cross — 9 June 1865 — POLICE COURT.—Thursday. [Before T. Beckham, Esq., R.M.] DRUNKENNESS. at <http://paperspast.natlib.govt.nz/cgi-bin/paperspast?a=d&d=DSC18650609.2.19&cl=search&srpos=8&e=--1865---1865--100--1--on--0%22lancashire+witch%22-ARTICLE->
142. The Daily Southern Cross. Three disobedient seamen. 9 June 1865. *Daily Southern Cross* 4 (1865).
143. Papers Past — Daily Southern Cross — 19 June 1865 — Saturday. [Before Dr. Horne, J. P., and D. B. Thornton, Esq., J. P.]. at <http://paperspast.natlib.govt.nz/cgi-bin/paperspast?a=d&cl=search&d=DSC18650619.2.31.1&srpos=21&e=--1865---1865--100--1--on--0%22lancashire+witch%22-ARTICLE->
144. Police Court.—friday. Desertions Lancashire Witch. 10 June 1865. *New Zealand Herald* 6 (1865).
145. Police Court.—tuesday. Desertions from the Lancashire Witch. 7 June 1865. *New Zealand Herald* 3 (1865).
146. Police Court.—monday. George Helmers and Henry Geo. Page. 20 June 1865. *New Zealand Herald* 5 (1865).
147. Papers Past — Daily Southern Cross — 21 June 1865 — POLICE COURT.—Tuesday. [Before Dr. Horne, J P, and D. Graham, Esq., J.P.] DRUNKENNESS. at <http://paperspast.natlib.govt.nz/cgi-bin/paperspast?a=d&d=DSC18650621.2.22&cl=search&srpos=17&e=--1865---1865--100--1--on--0%22lancashire+witch%22-ARTICLE->
148. Police Court.—monday. Harbouring a seaman. 27 June 1865. *New Zealand Herald* 5 (1865).
149. Papers Past — Daily Southern Cross — 27 June 1865 — POLICE COURT.—Monday. [Before T Beckham, Esq., R M]. at <http://paperspast.natlib.govt.nz/cgi-bin/paperspast?a=d&cl=search&d=DSC18650627.2.18&srpos=66&e=--1865---1865--100--1--on--0%22lancashire+witch%22-ARTICLE->
150. Accident at the ship Lancashire Witch. 5 June 1865. *New Zealand Herald* 5 (1865).
151. Immigrants housed at Point Chevalier. 12 June 1865. *New Zealand Herald* 4 5 (1865).
152. General Cameron To The Governor. Sailor on Lancashire Witch falls down hold. 1 August 1865. *Daily Southern Cross* 4 (1865).
153. Papers Past — Daily Southern Cross — 21 September 1865 — INQUEST ON THE BODY FOUND IN THE HARBOUR. at <http://paperspast.natlib.govt.nz/cgi-bin/paperspast?a=d&d=DSC18650921.2.21&cl=search&srpos=64&e=--1865---1865--100--1--on--0%22lancashire+witch%22-ARTICLE->
154. Papers Past — Daily Southern Cross — 20 September 1865 — ARRIVAL OF THE 'QUEEN.' IMPORTANT NEWS FROM THE SOUTH. at <http://paperspast.natlib.govt.nz/cgi-bin/paperspast?a=d&cl=search&d=DSC18650920.2.13&srpos=185&e=--1865---1865--100--101--on--0%22lancashire+witch%22-ARTICLE->
155. Port Op Auckland. 10 July 1866. *Daily Southern Cross* 3 (1866).
156. Miscellaneous. Sea Breeze for Russell. 17 June 1865. *Daily Southern Cross* 4 (1865).

157. Russell. Election of Mr. Carleton. (Prom our own correspondent.) March 7. *Daily Southern Cross*, Volume XXII, Issue 2698, 10 March 1866, Page 5.
158. Papers Past — Daily Southern Cross — 19 June 1865 — RUSSELL. (FROM OUR OWN CORRESPONDENT.) June 14. at <http://paperspast.natlib.govt.nz/cgi-bin/paperspast?a=d&cl=search&d=DSC18650619.2.27&srpos=26&e=--1865---1865--100--1--on--0%22lancashire+witch%22-ARTICLE->
159. Miscellaneous. Ellen sails for Wangarei. 21 June 1865. *Daily Southern Cross* 4 (1865).
160. Pioneers Of The North. Mr and Mrs J. Hare. 5 May 1927. *Auckland Star* 8 (1927).
161. Papers Past — Daily Southern Cross — 7 October 1865 — PORT OF AUCKLAND. MISCELLANEOUS. at <http://paperspast.natlib.govt.nz/cgi-bin/paperspast?a=d&cl=search&d=DSC18651007.2.5.1&srpos=226&e=--1865---1865--100--201--on--0%22lancashire+witch%22-ARTICLE->
162. Arrival Of The Tawera. Lancashire Witch adorned with bunting. 2 August 1865. *New Zealand Herald* 4 (1865).
163. Auckland's Needs And Auckland's Members. Mrs H. Aspden. 11 July 1905. *Auckland Star* 4 (1905).
164. Golden Wedding. Mr and Mrs Harry Barton. 3 November 1944. *Auckland Star* 3 (1944).
165. Obituary. Mr. Henry Cheeseman. 15 July 1924. *Auckland Star* 8 (1924).
166. Birth, Death and Marriage Historical Records. at <https://www.bdmhistoricalrecords.dia.govt.nz/home/>
167. Obituary. Hannah Gwilliam. 26 April 1918. *Thames Star* 2 (1918).
168. Diamond Wedding. Mr and Mrs Hare. 23 December 1933. *Auckland Star* 6 (1933).
169. 64 Years Wed. Mr and Mrs Edward Hare. 14 July 1938. *Auckland Star* 7 (1938).
170. Old Colonists' Deaths. Mr. Joseph Hare. 2 April 1919. *New Zealand Herald* 10 (1919).
171. Obituary. Mr Joseph Hare. 3 April 1919. *Auckland Star* 7 (1919).
172. 65 Years Ago. Mr and Mrs E. Hare. 12 July 1939. *Auckland Star* 13 (1939).
173. Obituary. Mrs Mary Ann Harrison. 8 January 1944. *Auckland Star* 7 (1944).
174. Obituary. William Henry Jacobs. 22 September 1920. *Thames Star* 2 (1920).
175. The Passing Of The Pioneers. Death of Mrs Ann Jones. 17 December 1917. *Ohinemuri Gazette* 2 (1917).
176. Early Colonist's Death. Mrs. Ann Jones. 22 December 1917. *New Zealand Herald* 8 (1917).
177. Mr Peter Kernot. 19 May 1905. *Auckland Star* 4 (1905).
178. Obituary. Mrs. Elizabeth Kernot. 22 January 1934. *Auckland Star* 3 (1934).
179. Sixty Years Ago. Emigrants in Whangarei. 9 June 1925. *Northern Advocate* 7 (1925).
180. Pukekohe | NZETC. M. B. Routly. at <http://nzetc.victoria.ac.nz/tm/scholarly/tei-Cyc02Cycl-t1-body1-d3-d2-d9.html#name-425874-mention>
181. Obituary. Mr. W. H. Saies. 7 February 1929. *Auckland Star* 17 (1929).
182. Death Of Mr. N. J. Sarah. 5 June 1894. *New Zealand Herald* 3 (1894).
183. Personal. Mrs N. J. Sarah. 20 September 1918. *Northern Advocate* 2 (1918).
184. Mr. John Sarah. 15 July 1929. *Auckland Star* 5 (1929).
185. Okaiawa. Mr and Mrs Taylor. 6 July 1909. *Hawera & Normanby Star* 3 (1909).
186. Personal Items. Richard Henry Taylor. 4 February 1918. *Hawera & Normanby Star* 4 (1918).
187. Obituary. Mr. Arthur Thomas. 16 May 1927. *Auckland Star* 8 (1927).
188. Obituary. Mrs Fanny Worth. 3 October 1921. *New Zealand Herald* 6 (1921).
189. Arrival Of The Ship Lancashire Witch. 30 July 1867. *Press* 2 (1867).
190. 'The Ship Lancashire Witch, 1574 Tons Register, Sailed Recently from London for Canterbury, New Zealand, with a Full Complement of Cabin Passengers, and about 110 in the Steerage.' Illustrated London News [London, England] 27 Apr. 1867: 427. Illustrated London News. Web. 6 June 2013.
191. Ross Winans - inventor of cigar ship. *Wikipedia, the free encyclopedia* (2013). at <http://en.wikipedia.org/w/index.php?title=Ross_Winans&oldid=546386450>
192. Shipping. Arrival of the Lancashire Witch. 3 August 1867. *Lyttelton Times* 2 (1867).
193. List Of Assisted Government Immigrants. Lancashire Witch. 30 July 1867. *Press* 2 (1867).
194. Port Of Onehunga. 3 September 1867. *New Zealand Herald* 3 (1867).
195. Town And Country. J. Millett charged with assaulting F. Wiggins on the Lancashire Witch. 5 August 1867. *Lyttelton Times* 2 3 (1867).
196. Christchurch. 3 August 1867. *Timaru Herald* 3 (1867).
197. Commissioners report on Lancashire Witch. 12 August 1867. *Lyttelton Times* 2 (1867).

198. Monthly Shipping List. 31 August 1867. *Timaru Herald* 2 (1867).
199. Immigration Commissioner to Provincial Secretary - Immigration reports, including (Light Brigade) 622a of 10/06/1868 (Gainsborough), 1865 of 30/12/1867, 1501 of 4/10/1867 (Blue Jacket), 1501.1, 1387 of 5/09/1867 (Lancashire Witch), 1095 of 5/07/1867 (Lincoln), 323 of 5/03/1867 (Himalaya), 84 of 18/01/1867 (Mermaid), 1733 of 17/11/1866 (Blue Jacket), 1345 of 6/09/1866, 1263 of 18/08/1866, 1117 of 18/07/1866 (John Temperley), 937 of 15/06/1866, 780 of 16/05/1866, 637 of 29/04/1866, 290 of 13/02/1866, 112 of 16/01/1866, 1894 of 14/12/1865, 1708 of 17/11/1865, 1531 of 14/10/1865, 1388 of 16/09/1965, 1201 of 12/08/1865 (Indian Empire), 1021 of 14/07/1865, 834 of 14/06/1865 (Greyhound), 676 of 16/05/1865, 636 of 8/05/1865, 365 of 14/03/1865 (Eastern Empire), 76.1, 2815 of 31/12/1864, 2814 of 31/12/1864 (British Empire), 2382 of 13/10/1864, 2381 of 13/10/1864, 1950 of 22/07/1864 (Amoor and Ivanhoe) - 5/09/1868 (R17559820). Christchurch office. Archives New Zealand.
200. J. Marshman (Emigration) to Provincial Secretary - press notices ?Lancashire Witch? 19/06/1867 (R22198188) Christchurch Office. Archives New Zealand.
201. Telegrams. Lancashire Witch for Callao. 19 October 1867. *Press* 2 (1867).
202. Shipping. 19 October 1867. *Lyttelton Times* 2 (1867).
203. Shipping. Lancashire Witch reached Callao in 37 days. 28 January 1868. *Lyttelton Times* 2 (1868).
204. Taonga, N. Z. M. for C. and H. T. M. Swift, Anne. at <http://www.teara.govt.nz/en/biographies/1s30/swift-anne>
205. Town And Country. Annie Swift convicted. 12 August 1867. *Lyttelton Times* 2 (1867).
206. Resident Magistrates' Courts. Annie Swift. 20 June 1868. *Press* 2 (1868).
207. Resident Magistrate's Court. Charles Massey charged. Anne Carte. 16 June 1870. *Press* 3 (1870).
208. Police Court.—friday. 5 March 1870. *New Zealand Herald* 6 (1870).
209. Police Court.—yesterday. Annie Swift alias Benson. 21 May 1875. *Thames Advertiser* 3 (1875).
210. Papers Past — Daily Southern Cross — 27 July 1876 — POLICE COURT.—Wednesday. [Before A. Beetham and George Donne, Esqs., J.P.'s.]. at <http://paperspast.natlib.govt.nz/cgi-bin/paperspast?a=d&cl=search&d=DSC18760727.2.22&srpos=9&e=-------100--1--on--0%22anne+swift%22-->
211. Another Fire In Chapel-street. 21 December 1878. *New Zealand Herald* 5 (1878).
212. Police Court.-this Day. Annie Swift alias Crochet. 17 January 1882. *Auckland Star* 2 (1882).
213. Police Court—this Day. 25 April 1888. *Auckland Star* 5 (1888).
214. Accidents, Etc. John Cooper. Annie Swift. 24 February 1890. *New Zealand Herald* 10 (1890).
215. Police Court—this Day. Ann Swift alias Cooper. 8 January 1903. *Auckland Star* 2 (1903).
216. Dr. Donald, Immigration Commission to Provincial Secretary - Report on 'Lancashire Witch' a few of the single females pregnant or with venereal disease. Filed with 1273(1), 1273(1) - 10/08/1867. (R23797993) Christchurch Office. Archives New Zealand.
217. Marshman (Emigration) to Provincial Secretary - surprised at report on the single women on the ?Lancashire Witch? 25/11/1867 (R22198560). Christchurch Office. Archives New Zealand.
218. Magistrates' Courts. Lizzie Daniels. 1 November 1867. *Lyttelton Times* 2 3 (1867).
219. The Press. Saturday, September 28, 1867. Lizzie Daniels. *Press* 2 (1867).
220. Resident Magistrate's Court. Lizzie Daniels. 9 November 1867. *Press* 3 (1867).
221. Supreme Court. Lizzie Feast. 4 April 1883. *Star* 3 (1883).
222. Deaths. Flora Georgina Smith 16 May 1930. *Auckland Star* 1 (1930).
223. Miscellaneous Wires. Samuel Derbridge. 2 July 1908. *Nelson Evening Mail* 4 (1908).
224. Confession Of Murder. Hester Hoskin. 4 March 1868. *Lyttelton Times* 7 (1868).
225. Singular Confession Of Murder. Hester Hoskin. 14 March 1868. *Marlborough Express* 5 (1868).
226. The Story Of Esther Hoskin. 25 July 1868. *Star* 3 (1868).
227. Social And Domestic. Hester Hoskin. 3 April 1868. *North Otago Times* 4 (1868).
228. Magisterial. Catherine Gilchrist. 28 October 1868. *Star* 3 (1868).
229. Crew of Lancashire Witch charged with abusive language. 18 October 1867. *Press* 2 (1867).
230. Obituary. Mr. Isaac Coates. 2 May 1932. *Auckland Star* 3 (1932).
231. Fatal Accident in the Avon. Charles Fowles. The Press. Tuesday, August 20, 1867. *Press* 2 (1867).

232. Clothiers, Dyers, Hatters, Etc | NZETC. Davis. at <http://nzetc.victoria.ac.nz//tm/scholarly/tei-Cyc01Cycl-t1-body-d4-d42-d2.html>
233. Town & Country. Hinman Jackson. 30 November 1899. *Timaru Herald* 2 (1899).
234. Personal Items. Edgar Jones. 20 October 1933. *Evening Post* 11 (1933).
235. Professional, Commercial And Industrial | NZETC. Gordon Parker Wood. at <http://nzetc.victoria.ac.nz/tm/scholarly/tei-Cyc03Cycl-t1-body1-d7-d1-d22.html#name-420591-mention>
236. Hughes, H. C. *Discharged in New Zealand: soldiers of the Imperial Foot regiments who took their discharge in New Zealand, 1840-1870.*
237. New Zealand, Immigration Passenger Lists, 1855-1973 Image New Zealand, Immigration Passenger Lists, 1855-1973; pal:/MM9.3.1/TH-266-11666-138666-24 — FamilySearch.org. 1863 passenger list. at <https://familysearch.org/pal:/MM9.3.1/TH-266-11666-138666-24?cc=1609792&wc=M9WV-8LT:1621907955>
238. Local And General News. James, Ann, Elizabeth and Jane Baker. 7 June 1915. *New Zealand Herald* 4 (1915).
239. New Zealand, Immigration Passenger Lists, 1855-1973 Image New Zealand, Immigration Passenger Lists, 1855-1973; pal:/MM9.3.1/TH-266-11019-64874-28 — FamilySearch.org. at <https://familysearch.org/pal:/MM9.3.1/TH-266-11019-64874-28?cc=1609792&wc=M9WV-818:n843446748>
240. Shipping. Cabin Passenger list. 30 July 1867. *Press* 2 (1867).

www.ingramcontent.com/pod-product-compliance
Lightning Source LLC
Chambersburg PA
CBHW050640160426
43194CB00010B/1752